C000070963

GET BY
LATIN AMERICAN
SPANISH

TATIANA SUAREZ
MARISOL DE LAFUENTE
SIMON CALDER

BBC Active, an imprint of Educational Publishers LLP, part of the Pearson Education Group
Edinburgh Gate, Harlow, Essex CM20 2JE, England
© Educational Publishers LLP 2008
BBC logo © BBC 1996. BBC and BBC ACTIVE are trademarks of the British Broadcasting
Corporation

First edition published 1998. This edition published 2008.

ISBN: 978-1-4066-4274-2

Cover concept design: Emma Wallace
Cover photograph: LMR Group/Alamy
Insides concept design: Nicolle Thomas
Layout: Pantek Arts Ltd. (www.pantekarts.co.uk)
Publisher: Debbie Marshall
Project editor: Emma Brown
Senior production controller: Franco Forgione
Marketing: Fiona Griffiths

Audio producer for the new edition: Martin Williamson, Prolingua Productions
Sound engineering: Studio AVP
Original audio producer: John Green, tefl tapes
Original sound engineer and music: Tim Woolf

Printed and bound in the UK by Ashford Colour Press Ltd.
The Publisher's policy is to use paper manufactured from sustainable forests.

All photographs supplied by Alamy Images.
p8 David Noton Photography; p10 Rubens Abboud; p15 J Marshall, Tribaleye Images;
p17 Les Polders; p23 Crispin Rodwell; p24 Simon Vine; p27 Lightworks Media;
p30 J Marshall, Tribaleye Images; p32 Beren Patterson; p35 Wendy Connett; p41 Mireille
Vautier; p44 Oliver Gerhard; p46 Bill Bachmann; p50 Javier Etcheverry; p55 Dan Herrick;
p59 Gary Cook; p61 Rachael Bowes; p64 Robert Fried; p71 Rubens Abboud; p72 Yadid
Levy; p74 Bon Appetit; p78 AM Corporation; p83 Angelo Cavalli; p88 Danita Delimont;
p90 R1; p96 Corey Wise; p100 Danita Delimont; p102 Wendy Connett; p105 Melvyn
Longhurst; p108 nagelestock.com; p114 Peter M. Wilson; p116 Melvyn Longhurst;
p124 Melvyn Longhurst

Contents

How to use this book

Get By in Latin American Spanish is divided into colour-coded topics to help you find what you need quickly. Each unit contains practical travel tips, and a phrasemaker to help you say what you need to and understand what you hear.

As well as listing key phrases, Get By in Latin American Spanish aims to help you understand how the language works so that you can start to communicate independently. The check out dialogues show the language in action and the try it out activities give you an opportunity to practise for yourself. The link up sections pick out the key structures and give helpful notes about their use. A round-up of all the basic grammar can be found in the Language Builder, pp130–136.

In Spanish, all nouns – things, people, concepts – are either masculine or feminine and this affects the way they are written and pronounced, as well as the words related to them. In the book these alternative endings are shown: masculine/feminine e.g. amigo/a (male friend/female friend.)

Some vocabulary varies from one Latin American country to another; the symbol † next to a word indicates that alternative translations are listed in the dictionary at the back of the book.

If you've bought the pack with the audio CD, you'll be able to listen to a selection of the most important phrases and check out dialogues, as well as all the as if you were there activities.

sounds Spanish

Written and spoken Spanish are very similar; each letter is usually pronounced in the same way each time you see it. It also helps that the pronunciation of many letters is very similar to English. This book uses a pronunciation guide, based on English sounds, to help you start speaking Spanish. Key points are also highlighted in the sound check sections.

vowels

	sounds like ...	shown as ...
a	'a' in 'man'	a
e	'e' in 'pen'	e/eh
i	'ee' in 'seem'	ee
o	'o' in 'hot'	o

u	'oo' in 'root'	oo
u (before another vowel)	'w' in 'wet'	w
u in que, qui, gue, gui	not pronounced	
ai, ay	'i' in 'tiny'	iy
au	'ow' in 'owl'	ow
ei, ey	'ay' in 'play'	ay
eu	the vowel sounds in 'hey you'	eoo
ia	'ya ' in 'yard'	ya
ie	'ye' in 'yes'	ye
io	'yo' in 'yoga'	yo
oi, oy	'oy' in 'boy'	oy

consonants

Many Spanish consonants are pronounced in much the same way as in English. Exceptions are listed below:

	sounds like ...	shown as ...
c + e/i	s	s
ch	'tch' in 'notch'	tch
d (only at end of word)	'th' in 'this'	th
g + e/i	a guttural 'h' as in Scottish 'loch'	hh
h	always silent	
j	a guttural 'h' as in Scottish 'loch'	hh
ll	'y' in 'yes'	y
ll (Argentina)	's' in 'leisure'	zh
ñ	'ni' in 'onion'	ny
q (always followed by u)	'k' in 'key'	k
r (usually)	lightly rolled	r
r (at beginning of word)	strongly rolled	rr
rr	strongly rolled	rr
v	'b' in 'bill'	b

x (at beginning of word and before a consonant)	's' in 'see'	s
x (between two vowels)	'x' in 'exit'	ks
x (in some words)	a guttural 'h' as in Scottish 'loch'	hh
y (on its own)	'ee' in 'seem'	ee
y (Argentina, except at end of word)	's' in 'leisure'	zh
z	's' in 'see'	s

variations

The key difference in the pronunciation of Spanish spoken in Spain is in the pronunciation of **ce**, **ci** and **z**, which sound like the 'th' in 'thin'.

stress

The part of a word stressed tends to follow different patterns in Spanish than in English. Stress is shown in this book in bold italics.

* If the word has a written accent, always put the stress on that part of the word: estación *esta**syon***
* If the word ends in a vowel, **n** or **s**, always stress the next to the last syllable: oficina *ofee**see**na*   cierran ***sye**rran*   correos *ko**rre**os*
* If the word ends in a consonant other than **n** or **s**, always stress the last syllable: azul *a**sool***   total *to**tal***   doctor *doc**tor***

alphabet

Here's a guide to how Latin Americans pronounce the alphabet:

A	*a*	B	*beh*	C	*seh*	D	*deh*
E	*eh*	F	***eh**ffeh*	G	*hheh*	H	*at**cheh*
I	*ee*	J	*hhota*	K	*ka*	L	*ehleh*
LL	***eh**yeh*	M	***eh**meh*	N	*ehneh*	Ñ	*eh**nyeh*
O	*oh*	P	*peh*	Q	*koo*	R	*eh**rreh*
S	***eh**sseh*	T	*teh*	U	*oo*	V	*beh-**kor**ta*
W	***do**bleh beh*	X	***eh**kees*	Y	*ee-**grye**ga*	Z	*seh**ta*

6

Bare **Necessities**

countries

Latin America includes the region of the Americas where Spanish and Portuguese are primarily spoken. This book covers those countries whose main language is Spanish: Argentina, Bolivia, Chile, Colombia, Costa Rica, Cuba, the Dominican Republic, Ecuador, El Salvador, Guatemala, Honduras, Mexico, Nicaragua, Panama, Paraguay, Peru, Puerto Rico, Uruguay and Venezuela.

currency

Each Latin American country has its own currency, although in some border towns two or more local currencies are accepted; exchange rates may fluctuate considerably according to the state of the country's economy.

You can change foreign currency at banks and **casas de cambio** (authorised bureaux de change) in most major cities. The US dollar is the most widely accepted currency, but Euros are becoming increasingly common. If you are visiting rural or remote places, it is advisable to carry a reasonable amount of cash in small notes. Cash points (**ATM**) are common in larger urban areas and accept major foreign debit cards. Credit cards are generally accepted in higher-priced establishments in major cities but elsewhere their use is limited. Bear in mind that US credit cards are not welcome in Cuba.

greeting people

Latin American people are generally warm and friendly, so you can use first names after being introduced. In a formal/business situation, you should address someone as **Señor** (for a man) or **Señora** (for a woman).

Emphasis is placed on courtesy when talking to strangers. You should greet someone in a public establishment with **buenos días, buenas tardes** or **buenas noches** ('good morning', 'good afternoon' or 'good evening') and always use the words 'please' (**por favor**) and 'thank you' (**gracias**).

phrasemaker

greetings
you may say ...

Hello!	¡Hola!	*ola*
Good morning.	Buenos días.	*bwenos deeas*
Good afternoon/ evening.	Buenas tardes.	*bwenas tardes*
Good evening/night.	Buenas noches.	*bwenas notches*
See you later.	Hasta luego/Nos vemos.	*asta lwego/nos bemos*
See you tomorrow.	Hasta mañana/Nos vemos mañana.	*asta manyana/nos bemos manyana*
Bye.	Adiós.	*adyos*
How are you?	¿Cómo está?	*komo esta*
(Very) well, thank you, and you?	(Muy) bien, gracias, ¿y usted?	*(mwee) byen grasyas, ee oosteth*

other useful words
you may say ...

please	por favor	*por fabor*
Thank you (very much).	(Muchas) gracias.	*(mootchas) grasyas*
You're welcome.	De nada.	*deh nada*
Excuse me.	Con permiso.	*kon permeeso*
Sorry.	Perdón/Perdone.	*perdon/perdoneh*
Have a good time!	¡Que le vaya bien!	*keh leh baya byen*

Bare **Necessities**

Have a good trip!	¡Buen viaje!	*bwen **byah**heh*
Have a nice meal!	¡Buen provecho!	*bwen pro**bet**cho*
Cheers!	¡Salud!	*sal**ooth***
Here you are.	Aquí tiene.	*a**kee tye**neh*
okay	bueno.	***bwe**no*
It doesn't matter.	No importa.	*no eem**por**ta*
Of course!	¡Claro!	***kla**ro*
yes/no	sí/no	*see/no*
sir/madam	señor/señora	*se**nyor**/sen**yo**ra*
Can I (come in)?	¿Se puede pasar?	*seh **pwe**de pa**sar***

about yourself
you may say …

My name is …	Me llamo …	*meh **ya**mo*
I'm from …, and you?	Soy de … ¿y usted?	*soy deh … ee oos**teth***
I live in …	Vivo en …	***bee**bo en*
I'm …	Soy …	*soy*
a lawyer.	abogado/a.	*abo**ga**do/a*
a teacher.	profesor/a.	*profe**sor**/a*
an engineer.	ingeniero/a.	*eenhhen**ye**ro/a*
a student.	estudiante.	*estoo**dyan**teh*
I study economics.	Estudio economía.	*es**too**dyo ehkono**mee**a*
I work in an office.	Trabajo en una oficina	*tra**bah**ho en **oo**na ofee**see**na*
I'm …	Estoy …	*es**toy***
single.	soltero/a.	*sol**te**ro/a*
married.	casado/a.	*ka**sa**do/a*
divorced.	divorciado/a.	*deebor**sya**do/a*
I'm …	Soy …	*soy*
Irish.	irlandés (man).	*eerlan**des***
(see nationalities, p16)	irlandesa (woman).	*eerlan**de**sa*
I'm … years old. (see numbers, p14)	Tengo … años.	***ten**go … **an**yos*
I have … children.	Tengo … hijos.	***ten**go … **eeh**hos*
I don't have children.	No tengo hijos.	*no **ten**go **eeh**hos*

I'm here on holiday/ business.	Estoy aquí de vacaciones/negocios.	*estoy akee deh bakasyones/negosyos*
So am I.	Yo también.	*yo tambyen*
I'm staying for a week.	Paso una semana aquí.	*paso oona semana akee*
I speak a little Spanish.	Hablo un poco de español.	*ablo oon poko deh espanyol*
Pleased to meet you.	Mucho gusto.	*mootcho goosto*

about other people

you may say ...

What's your name?	¿Cómo se llama?	*komo seh yama*
This is ...	Este es ...	*esteh es ...*
Mr ...	el señor ...	*el senyor*
my husband.	mi esposo.	*mee esposo*
my colleague.	mi colega.	*mee kolega*
my friend. (male)	mi amigo.	*mee ameego*
This is ...	Esta es ...	*esta es*
Mrs ...	la señora ...	*la senyora*
my wife.	mi esposa.	*mee esposa*
my friend. (female)	mi amiga.	*mee ameega*
Where are you from?	¿De dónde es usted?	*deh dondeh es oosteth*
Are you English?	¿Es usted inglés/esa?	*es oosteth eengles/esa*
What do you do for a living?	¿En qué trabaja?	*en keh trabahha*
Do you speak English?	¿Habla inglés?	*abla eengles*
Are you travelling alone?	¿Viaja solo/a?	*byahha solo/a*
I'm with ...	Estoy con ...	*estoy kon*
my family.	mi familia.	*mee fameelya*
friends.	amigos.	*ameegos*
Are you here on holiday?	¿Está usted aquí de vacaciones?	*esta oosteth akee deh bakasyones*

Bare **Necessities**

How long are you staying for?	¿Cuánto tiempo se queda?	*kwanto tyempo seh keda*

useful phrases
you may say ...

Is there a lift?	¿Hay ascensor†?	*iy asensor*
Are there any toilets?	¿Hay baños?	*iy banyos*
Where is the main square?	¿Dónde está la plaza†?	*dondeh esta la plasa*
Where are the shops?	¿Dónde están las tiendas†?	*dondeh estan las tyendas*
Do you have a room?	¿Tiene un cuarto/una habitación?	*tyeneh oon kwartol oona abeetasyon*
Do you have any ice cream?	¿Tiene helados?	*tyeneh elados*

I'd like ...
  a kilo of oranges.
	Quisiera ...
	  un kilo de naranjas.
		keesyera
		  oon keelo deh naranhhas

How much does it cost?	¿Cuánto cuesta?	*kwanto kwesta*
How much is a kilo of tomatoes?	¿Cuánto cuesta un kilo de tomates?	*kwanto kwesta oon keelo deh tomates*
How much do they cost?	¿Cuánto cuestan?	*kwanto kwestan*
How much are the earrings?	¿Cuánto cuestan los aretes?	*kwanto kwestan los aretes*

getting things straight ...
you may say ...

Pardon?	¿Cómo?	*komo*
Could you say that again, please?	¿Puede repetir, por favor?	*pwedeh repeteer por fabor*
More slowly, please.	Más despacio, por favor.	*mas despasyo por fabor*
How do you spell it?	¿Cómo se escribe?	*komo seh eskreebeh*
Will you write it for me, please?	¿Me lo puede escribir, por favor?	*meh lo pwede eskreebeer por fabor*

check out 1

At the hotel reception you run into an Argentinian guest you met briefly the day before.

- ¡Hola! Buenos días
  ola. bwenos deeyas

- Buenos días. ¿Cómo está?
  bwenos deeyas. komo esta

- Muy bien, ¿y usted?
  mwee byen. ee oosteth

- Bien, gracias.
  byen grasyas

- Esta es mi esposa Isabel.
  esta es mee esposa eesabel

- Mucho gusto.
  mootcho goosto

- Bueno, adiós. ¡Hasta luego!
  bweno adyos. asta lwego

- Adiós. ¡Que le vaya bien!
  adyos. keh leh baya byen

Q Who did the guest introduce to you?
What did the guest wish you?

changing money

you may say ...

I'd like to change ...	Quisiera cambiar ...	*keesyera kambyar*
£100.	cien libras.	*syen leebras*
$50.	cincuenta dólares.	*seenkwenta dolares*
traveller's cheques.	cheques de viajero.	*tchekes deh byahhero*
What is the exchange rate?	¿A cómo está el cambio?	*a komo esta el kambyo*

Bare **Necessities**

What is the pound/ dollar at?	¿A cómo está la libra/el dólar?	*a komo esta la leebra/ el dolar*
What's the commission charge?	¿Cuánto es la comisión?	*kwanto es la komeesyon*

you may hear ...

¿Tiene su pasaporte, por favor?	*tyeneh soo pasaporteh por fabor*	Can I see your passport, please?
La libra está a (trece) pesos.	*la leebra esta a (treseh) pesos*	The pound is at (13) pesos.

the time

What time is it?	¿Qué hora es?	*keh ora es*
What time does it ... open/close? leave/arrive?	¿A qué hora ... abre/cierra? sale/llega?	*a keh ora abreh/syerra saleh/ yega*
It's ... one o'clock. five past one.	Es ... la una. la una y cinco.	*es la oona la oona ee seenko*
midday midnight	mediodía medianoche	*medyodeea medyanotcheh*
It's ... two. a quarter past five. (twenty) past seven.	Son ... las dos. las cinco y cuarto. las siete y (veinte).	*son las dos las seenko ee kwarto las syeteh ee (baynteh)*
It's a quarter to eight.	Es un cuarto para las ocho.[1]	*es oon kwarto para las otcho*
It's ... ten/five to six in the afternoon/ evening. five to one in the morning.	Son ... diez/cinco para las seis de la tarde. cinco para la una de la mañana.[2]	*son dyes/seenko para las says deh la tardeh seenko para la oona deh la manyana*
At half past (eleven) at night.	A las (once) y media de la noche.	*a las (onseh) ee medya deh la notcheh*

[1]Argentina: Son las ocho menos cuarto. *son las otcho menos kwarto*
[2]Argentina: Es la una menos cinco de la mañana. *es la oona menos seenko deh la manyana*

numbers

0	cero	*sehro*
1	un/uno/una*	*oon/oono/oona*
2	dos	*dos*
3	tres	*tres*
4	cuatro	*kwatro*
5	cinco	*seenko*
6	seis	*says*
7	siete	*syeteh*
8	ocho	*otcho*
9	nueve	*nwebeh*
10	diez	*dyes*
11	once	*onseh*
12	doce	*doseh*
13	trece	*treseh*
14	catorce	*katorseh*
15	quince	*keenseh*
16	dieciséis	*dyeseesays*
17	diecisiete	*dyeseesyeteh*
18	dieciocho	*dyesyotcho*
19	diecinueve	*dyeseenwebeh*
20	veinte	*baynteh*
21	veintiuno	*bayntyoono*
22	veintidós	*baynteedos*
23	veintitrés	*baynteetres*
24	veinticuatro	*baynteekwatro*

25	veinticinco	*baynteeseenko*
26	veintiséis	*baynteesays*
27	veintisiete	*baynteesyeteh*
28	veintiocho	*bayntyotcho*
29	veintinueve	*baynteenwebeh*
30	treinta	*traynta*
40	cuarenta	*kwarenta*
50	cincuenta	*seenkwenta*
51	cincuenta y uno	*seenkwenta ee oono*
60	sesenta	*sesenta*
62	sesenta y dos	*sesenta ee dos*
70	setenta	*setenta*
73	setenta y tres	*setenta ee tres*
80	ochenta	*otchenta*
90	noventa	*nobenta*
100	cien	*syen*
101	ciento uno	*syento oono*
110	ciento diez	*syento dyes*
200	doscientos	*dosyentos*
293	doscientos noventa y tres	*dosyentos nobenta ee tres*
300	trescientos	*tresyentos*
500	quinientos	*keenyentos*
600	seiscientos	*saysyentos*
700	setecientos	*setesyentos*
800	ochocientos	*otchosyentos*

900	novecientos	*nobesyentos*
1,000	mil	*meel*
1,284	mil doscientos ochenta y cuatro	*meel dosyentos otchenta ee kwatro*
2,000	dos mil	*dos meel*

(*el número uno = number one, un sombrero = a hat,
una naranja = an orange)

check out 2

You walk into a *Casa de Cambio* to change money.

– Buenos días.
   bwenos deeas

○ Buenos días. ¿A cómo está la libra?
   bwenos deeyas. a komo esta la leebra

– Está a ... diez pesos.
   esta a ... dyes pesos

○ Bueno. Quisiera cambiar cheques de viajero, cien libras.
   bweno. keesyera kambyar tchekes deh byahhero, syen leebras

– Sí señor. ¿Tiene su pasaporte, por favor?
   see senyor. tyeneh soo pasaporteh por fabor

○ Aquí tiene.
   akee tyeneh

Q Roughly how many pesos will you get for your money?
What did the assistant ask you for?

ordinal numbers

1st	primero/a	*preemero/a*
2nd	segundo/a	*segoondo/a*
3rd	tercero/a	*tersero/a*
4th	cuarto/a	*kwarto/a*
5th	quinto/a	*keento/a*
6th	sexto/a	*sesto/a*
7th	séptimo/a	*septeemo/a*
8th	octavo/a	*oktabo/a*
9th	noveno/a	*nobeno/a*
10th	décimo/a	*deseemo/a*

countries and nationalities

Argentina: Argentinian	Argentina: argentino/a	*arhhenteena: arhhenteeno/a*
Australia: Australian	Australia: australiano/a	*owstralya: owstralyano/a*
Belize: Belizean	Belice: beliceño/a	*beleeseh: beleesenyo/a*
Bolivia: Bolivian	Bolivia: boliviano/a	*boleebya: boleebyano/a*
Brazil: Brazilian	Brasil: brasileño/a brasilero/a	*braseel: braseelenyo/a braseelero/a*
Canada: Canadian	Canadá: canadiense	*kanada: kanadyenseh*
Chile: Chilean	Chile: chileno/a	*tcheeleh: tcheeleno/a*
Colombia: Colombian	Colombia: colombiano/a	*kolombya: kolombyano/a*
Costa Rica: Costa Rican	Costa Rica: costarricense	*kosta rreeka: kostarreesenseh*
Cuba: Cuban	Cuba: cubano/a	*kooba: koobano/a*
Dominican Republic: Dominican	República Dominicana: dominicano/a	*rrepoobleeka domeeneekana: domeeneekano/a*
Ecuador: Ecuadorian	Ecuador: ecuatoriano/a	*ekwador: ekwatoryano/a*
El Salvador: Salvadorian	El Salvador: salvadoreño/a	*el salbador: salbadorenyo/a*

England: English	Inglaterra: inglés/esa	*eenglaterra: eengles/esa*
Guatemala: Guatemalan	Guatemala: guatemalteco/a	*gwatemala: gwatemalteko/a*
Honduras: Honduran	Honduras: hondureño/a	*ondooras: ondoorenyo/a*
Ireland: Irish	Irlanda: irlandés/esa	*eerlanda: eerlandes/esa*
Mexico: Mexican	México: mexicano/a	*mehheeko: mehheekano/a*
New Zealand: New Zealander	Nueva Zelanda: neozelandés/esa	*nweba selanda: neoselandes/esa*
Nicaragua: Nicaraguan	Nicaragua: nicaragüense	*neekaragwa: neekaragwense*
Northern Ireland: Northern Irish	Irlanda del Norte: norirlandés/esa	*eerlanda del norteh: noreerlandes/esa*
Panama: Panamanian	Panamá: panameño/a	*panama: panamenyo/a*
Paraguay: Paraguayan	Paraguay: paraguayo/a	*paragwiy: paragwiyo/a*
Peru: Peruvian	Perú: peruano/a	*peroo: perwano/a*
Puerto Rico: Puerto Rican	Puerto Rico: puertorriqueño/a portorriqueño/a	*pwerto rreeko: pwertorreekenyo/a portorreekenyo/a*
Scotland: Scottish	Escocia: escocés/esa	*eskosya: eskoses/esa*
South Africa:	Sudáfrica/Suráfrica:	*soodafreeka/ soorafreeka:*
South African	sudafricano/a surafricano/a	*soodafreekano/a soorafreekano/a*
United States/America: American	los Estados Unidos/América/Norteamérica: estadounidense/americano/a/norteamericano/a	*los estados ooneedos/amereeka/norteh-amereeka: estado-ooneedenseh/amereekano/a/norteh-amereekano/a*
Uruguay: Uruguayan	Uruguay: uruguayo/a	*ooroogwiy: ooroogwiyo/a*

Venezuela: Venezuelan	Venezuela: venezolano/a	*beneswela: benesolano/a*
Wales: Welsh	Gales: galés/esa	*gales: gales/esa*

days

Monday	lunes	*loones*
Tuesday	martes	*martes*
Wednesday	miércoles	*myerkoles*
Thursday	jueves	*hhwebes*
Friday	viernes	*byernes*
Saturday	sábado	*sabado*
Sunday	domingo	*domeengo*
today/yesterday/ tomorrow	hoy/ayer/mañana	*oy/ayer/manyana*
tonight	esta noche	*esta notcheh*
last night	anoche	*anotcheh*
last/next Thursday	el jueves pasado/que viene	*el hhwebes pasado/ keh byeneh*
on Mondays	los lunes	*los loones*
this Saturday	el sábado/este sábado	*el sabado/este sabado*
(at) the weekend	el fin de semana	*el feen deh semana*

months

January	enero	*enero*
February	febrero	*febrero*
March	marzo	*marso*
April	abril	*abreel*
May	mayo	*mayo*
June	junio	*hhoonyo*
July	julio	*hhoolyo*
August	agosto	*agosto*
September	septiembre	*septyembreh*
October	octubre	*oktoobreh*
November	noviembre	*nobyembreh*
December	diciembre	*deesyembreh*

Bare **Necessities**

sound check

There are five basic vowel sounds in Spanish:

a	like the 'a' in 'man'	casa *ka*sa	nada *na*da
e	like the 'e' in 'pen'	trece *tre*seh	entre *en*treh
i	like the 'ee' in 'seem'	salida sa*lee*da	sí *see*
o	like the 'o' in 'hot'	por favor por fa*bor*
u	like the 'oo' in 'root'	mucho gusto *moo*tcho *goos*to

try it out

missing vowels

Say the numbers below out loud, using the letters as clues.

4 _____ ctr	8 _____ ch
10 _____ dz	16 _____ dcss
20 _____ vnt	50 _____ cncnt
90 _____ nvnt	100 _____ cn
300 _____ trscnts	1000 _____ ml

get it right

What do you say when you …

1 need to go to the toilet in a museum?
2 greet somebody at night?
3 are about to have a drink?
4 want to get past somebody blocking your way?
5 want to know the price of some earrings?
6 are going to the fifth floor and don't want to use the stairs?
7 have accidentally stepped on someone's foot?

as if you were there

You get talking to another passenger during your flight to Cancun. Follow the prompts to play your part.

¿Va a Cancún?

(Ask him to speak more slowly)

Cancún. ¿Va a Cancún?

(Say yes)

¿Es americana?

(Say you're English)

Soy del DF.

(Say 'Pardon?')

Del DF ... de la Ciudad de México, pero vivo en Cancún. Me llamo Andrés. Andrés Parra, ¿y usted?

(Tell him your name is Anna)

linkup

key phrases		
Me llamo ...	**My name is** ...
Soy inglés/inglesa.	**I'm** English.
Vivo en Londres.	**I live in** London.
Tengo tres hijos.	**I have** three children.
¿Hay baños?	**Are there** any toilets?
¿Hay ascensor?	**Is there** a lift?
¿Tiene naranjas?	**Do you have** any oranges?
Quisiera dos kilos.	**I'd like** two kilos.
¿Dónde está la estación?	**Where's** the station?

Bare **Necessities**

the way you say things

You can't always transfer things word for word from one language to another. Me llamo Simon literally means 'Myself (I) call Simon', so sometimes it pays to learn the whole phrase rather than the individual words.

listening and replying

When people ask you questions about yourself, such as ¿Tiene hijos? (Do you have children?), it's tempting to reply using the same word: tiene.

But instead, you change the form of the word, for example using **tengo** (I have) not **tiene** (you have):

Sí, tengo dos hijos/No, no tengo hijos.
Yes, I have children/No, I don't have children.

¿Dónde vive? – Vivo en Leeds.
Where do you live? – I live in Leeds.

missing words

Because the form of the verb tells you who is being referred to, it is very common not to use the words for 'I' (yo) or 'you' (usted) in Spanish.

Soy inglés. (not yo soy) I'm English.
¿Tiene hijos? (not tiene usted) Do you have children?

The same applies to the words for he, she and it (él and ella):

¿Cómo se llama tu hija? – Se llama Emma (not Ella se llama Emma) What's your daughter called? – She's called Emma.

¿Dónde está el ascensor? – Está a la derecha (not El está a la derecha) Where's the lift? – It's on the right.

For more on verbs, see the Language Builder, p132. ┄┄>

Getting **Around**

arriving by air

UK airlines operate direct or connecting flights to most Latin American countries, but the easiest way to travel from mainland Europe is via charter flights operated by French or Spanish airlines. Another option, especially if your destination is Central America, is to fly via the USA.

car hire

Most capitals have branches of international and local rental companies. To hire a car, you should be 25 or over, and have an international driving licence and credit card.

Driving in Latin America can be challenging, as local drivers tend to ignore regulations and road signs. Secure parking and theft from vehicles can also be a problem. Your passport, driving licence and vehicle documents should be carried at all times since police checks are common.

As an alternative to hiring a car,

consider hiring a local taxi driver at a daily rate, which is usually not much more expensive.

taxi

Taxis are plentiful and relatively inexpensive. Fares are mostly based on a distance or zone system but may also be negotiable, so make sure you fix a price before you set off. Some places have collective taxis (colectivos), which run along fixed routes

long-distance bus

Buses are extremely good value for long-distance travel. Quality varies both within and between countries; the best quality and most expensive (Pullman, primera clase or de lujo), are more comfortable, better equipped and more punctual. At the other end of the scale are flat-bedded lorries fitted with seats. These are likely to be overcrowded and stop frequently. Larger towns or cities will have

one or more terminals (**terminal de buses** or **terminal terrestre**), which are likely to be on the outskirts.

rail

Unfortunately, railways are in decline throughout the region. There are generally two or more classes of travel (tourist class is the most luxurious and expensive, second class is the most basic). Tourist class tickets can be bought through tour agencies; second class tickets are more difficult to obtain and can involve lengthy queues at the station.

air

Almost all countries have an internal airline network and, although it's often possible to book internal flights from home, it's cheaper to book in the country. Internet booking is still not widespread, so book through a local travel agent (a small fee might be involved). It's advisable to confirm your flight before travelling as overbooking and cancellations can be a problem. A domestic airport tax is payable before flying.

boat

In some regions this is the only way to get around without flying. Explore the Amazon backwaters by canoe or visit the Galápagos Islands and glaciers of Patagonia by tourist yacht or ship.

travellers with disabilities

This is not the easiest of destinations for disabled travellers. Local buses and coaches will probably prove difficult and you might need to settle for taxis and internal flights. Not even the most modern underground systems in big cities are fully wheelchair friendly. The more developed countries, Chile, Argentina and Mexico, are likely to be the most accessible.

phrasemaker

asking the way
you may say …

Excuse me.	Perdone.	*perdoneh*
Is there … near here?	¿Hay … por aquí?	*iy … por akee*
a bank	un banco	*oon banko*
a bus stop	una parada (de buses/de autobuses†)	*oona parada (deh booses/deh owtobooses)*
an internet café	un café internet/un cibercafé	*oon kafeh eenternet/oon seeber-kafeh*
a bureau de change	una casa de cambio	*oona kasa deh kambyo*
a petrol station	una gasolinera/una estación de servicio†	*oona gasoleenera/oona estasyon deh serbeesyo*
a cash point	un cajero automático	*oon kahhero owtomateeko*
Where is the … please?	¿Dónde está … por favor?	*dondeh esta … por fabor*
tourist office	la oficina de turismo	*la ofeeseena deh tooreesmo*
town centre	el centro	*el sentro*
Where are the …	¿Dónde están …	*dondeh estan*
stairs?	las escaleras?	*las eskaleras*
toilets?	los baños/los sanitarios?	*los banyos/los saneetaryos*

Getting **Around**

Is there wheelchair access?	¿Hay acceso para silla de ruedas?	*iy akseso para seeya deh rwedas*
I'm lost.	Estoy perdido.	*estoy perdeedo*

you may hear ...

You ask a passer-by for help.

○ ¿Perdone, dónde está el Museo Frida Kahlo?
perdoneh, dondeh esta el mooseo freeda kalo

– Derecho, a dos cuadras. En la esquina de Allende y Londres.
deretcho a dos kwadras. en la eskeena deh ayendeh ee londres

Q   Is the Frida Kahlo Museum far?

hiring a car or bike

you may say ...

I'd like to hire a ...	Quisiera alquilar	*keesyera alkeelar*
car.	un coche†.	*oon kotcheh*
bike.	una bicicleta.	*oona beeseekleta*
motorbike.	una moto.	*oona moto*
scooter.	una moto scooter.	*oona moto eskooter*
for ...	por ...	*por*
three days	tres días	*tres deeas*
a week	una semana	*oona semana*
How much is it per ...	¿Cuánto cuesta por ...	*kwanto kwesta por*
day?	día?	*deea*
week?	semana?	*semana*
a ... car	un coche ...	*oon kotcheh*
small	pequeño/chico	*pekenyo/tcheeko*
fairly big	bastante grande	*bastanteh grandeh*
three-door	coupé/cupé	*koopeh*
five-door	sedán	*sedan*
manual	mecánico	*mekaneeko*
automatic	automático	*owtomateeko*

Getting **Around**

Is the ... included?	¿Está incluido ... ?	esta eenklweedo
insurance	el seguro	el se**goo**ro
mileage	el kilometraje	el keelome**trah**heh
tax	el impuesto	el eem**pwes**to
petrol	la gasolina†	la gaso**lee**na
VAT	el IVA	el **ee**ba
Do I have to pay a deposit?	¿Tengo que pagar depósito?	**ten**go keh pa**gar** de**pos**eeto

¿Qué tipo?	keh **tee**po	What type?
¿Por cuánto tiempo?	por **kwan**to **tyem**po	For how long?
¿Quién va a manejar?	kyen ba a mane**hhar**	Who is driving?
Tenemos ... que hablan inglés.	te**nemos** ... keh **ablan** een**gles**	We have English-speaking ...
choferes	tcho**fe**res	drivers.
guías	**gee**as	guides.
quinientos pesos al día	kee**nyen**tos **pe**sos al **dee**a	five hundred pesos a day (see numbers, p14)
dos mil pesos a la semana	dos meel **pe**sos a la se**mana**	two thousand pesos a week
Es aparte.	es a**part**eh	It's extra.
Su licencia†, por favor.	soo lee**sen**sya, por fa**bor**	Your driving licence, please.
Tenga la llave.	**ten**ga la **ya**beh	Here's the key.

check out 2

You enquire about hiring a car.

○ Quisiera alquilar un coche pequeño.
  keesyera alkeelar oon kotcheh pekenyo

– Tenemos un sedán automático.
  tenemos un sedan owtomateeko

○ ¿Cuánto cuesta por semana?
  kwanto kwesta por semana

– Dos mil pesos, con seguro incluido.
  dos meel pesos kon segooro eenklweedo

○ ¿Tengo que pagar depósito?
  tengo keh pagar deposeeto

– Sí. Son sesenta pesos de depósito.
  see. son sesenta pesos deh deposeeto

(con = with)

Q How much is it to hire a five-door car for a week with the deposit?

some road signs
you may see ...

alto/pare	*alto/pareh*	stop
camino en reparación	*kameeno en reparasyon*	road works
ceda el paso	*seda el paso*	give way
conserve su derecha	*konserbeh soo deretcha*	keep right
cruce de caminos/ intersección de vías	*crooseh deh kameenos/ eenterseksyon deh beeas*	crossroads
cruce peatonal	*crooseh peatonal*	pedestrian crossing
despacio	*despasyo*	(go) slowly
desviación/desvío	*desbyasyon/desbeeo*	detour
disminuya su velocidad	*deesmeenooya soo beloseedath*	slow down

glorieta/rotonda	*gloryeta/rotonda*	roundabout
no hay paso/vía cerrada	*no iy paso/beea serrada*	no entry
peligro	*peleegro*	danger
prohibido estacionar†	*proeebeedo estasyonar*	no parking

getting petrol
you may say …

Fill it up, please.	Lleno, por favor.	*yeno por fabor*
30 litres of (unleaded) petrol	Treinta litros de gasolina (sin plomo)	*traynta leetros deh gasoleena (seen plomo)*
50 pesos of petrol please.	Cincuenta pesos de gasolina, por favor.	*seenkwenta pesos deh gasoleena por fabor*
Is it self-service?	¿Es autoservicio?	*es owto-serbeesyo*
Do you have … diesel? 4 star?	¿Hay … gasoil? Súper?	*iy gasoyl sooper*
Please could you check the … oil? water?	¿Por favor, puede revisar … el aceite? el agua?	*por fabor pwedeh rebeesar el asayteh el agwal*

you may hear …

¿Le reviso las llantas†?	*leh rebeeso las yantas*	Shall I check your tyres?
Están bien.	*estan byen*	They're OK.
Le falta aire.	*leh falta iyreh*	You need air.

on the road
you may say …

Is the road to Cuzco in good condition?	¿Está buena la carretera† a Cuzco?	*esta bwena la karretera a koosko*
Is this the road to Otavalo?	¿Es ésta la carretera a Otavalo?	*es esta la karretera a otabalo*

Do you have to pay a toll?	¿Hay que pagar peaje†?	*iy keh pagar peahheh*
Is Mérida far?	¿Está lejos Mérida?	*esta lehhos mereeda*
How far is Taxco?	¿Qué tan lejos está Taxco?	*keh tan lehhos esta tasko*
Can I park here?	¿Puedo estacionar aquí?	*pwedo estasyonar akee*
Where is the nearest car park?	¿Dónde está el estacionamiento más cercano?	*dondeh esta el estasyonamyento mas serkano*

you may hear ...

No, es un sendero†.	*no es oon sendero*	No, it's a track.
La carretera está mala.	*la karretera esta mala*	The road is bad.
Hay desvíos/obras.	*iy desbeeos/obras*	There are detours/ road works.
Sí, hay caseta(s)† de cobro.	*see iy kaseta(s) deh kobro*	Yes, there is/are (a) toll booth(s).
Está (como) a treinta kilómetros.	*esta (komo) a traynta keelometros*	It's (about) 30 kilometres away.

check out 3
You would like to drive to Puerto Escondido.

○ ¿Está buena la carretera a Puerto Escondido?
esta bwena la karretera a pwerto eskondeedo

– Sí, muy buena.
see, mwee bwena

○ ¿Está lejos Puerto Escondido?
esta lehhos pwerto eskondeedo

– No, como a ciento cincuenta kilómetros.
no, komo a syento seenkwenta keelometros

 Puerto Escondido is 150 kilometres away and the road is very good: true/false?

planning your journey

you may say ...

Are there ... to Bogotá?	¿Hay ... para Bogotá?	*iy ... para bogota*
coaches	autobuses	*owtobooses*
trains	trenes	*trenes*
planes	aviones	*abyones*
What time does the ferry to Bellavista leave?	¿A qué hora sale el ferry para Bellavista?	*a keh ora saleh el ferree para beyabeesta*
What time does the next one leave?	¿A qué hora sale el próximo?	*a keh ora saleh el prokseemo*
What time does it arrive?	¿A qué hora llega?	*a keh ora yega*
Which ... does it leave from?	¿De qué ... sale?	*deh keh ... saleh*
platform	andén†	*anden*
gate	puerta	*pwerta*

31

How long does it take?	¿Cuánto tarda?	*kwanto tarda*
Is it air conditioned?	¿Tiene aire acondicionado?	*tyeneh iyreh akondeesyonado*
Is food provided?	¿Sirven comida?	*seerben komeeda*
Does it have a toilet?	¿Tiene baño?	*tyeneh banyo*
Do you have a timetable?	¿Tiene un horario?	*tyeneh oon oraryo*

you may hear...

| Salen cada hora. | *salen kada ora* | They leave every hour. |
| Tarda (seis) horas. | *tarda (says) oras* | It takes (six) hours. |

(See p13 for more on telling the time.)

buying a ticket

you may say ...

Where is the ticket office?	¿Dónde está la taquilla?	*dondeh esta la takeeya*
A single ticket, please.	Un boleto de ida, por favor.	*oon boleto deh eeda, por fabor*
A return ticket to Mendoza.	Un boleto de ida y vuelta a Mendoza.	*oon boleto deh eeda ee bwelta a mendosa*
Which one is cheaper?	¿Cuál es el más barato?	*kwal es el mas barato*
Which one is faster?	¿Cuál es el más rápido?	*kwal es el mas rrapeedo*
two adults and one child	dos adultos y un niño	*dos adooltos ee oon neenyo*

Getting **Around**

I'd like to reserve a ...	Quisiera reservar ...	_keesyera reserbar_
seat.	un asiento.	_oon asyento_
couchette.	una alcoba.	_oona alkoba_
Is there a reduction for ...	¿Hay descuento para ... ?	_iy deskwento para_
students?	estudiantes	_estoodyantes_
children?	niños	_neenyos_
senior citizens?	pensionados	_pensyonados_
Can I pay with credit/debit card?	¿Puedo pagar con tarjeta de crédito/débito?	_pwedo pagar kon tarhheta deh kredeeto/debeeto_

you may hear...

Hay un cargo adicional de veinte pesos.	_iy oon kargo adeesyonal deh baynteh pesos_	**There is a supplement of 20 pesos.**

check out 4
You are thinking of taking a coach to Acapulco.

- ¿A qué hora hay autobuses para Acapulco?
  a keh ora iy owtobooses para akapoolko

– Salen cada hora.
  salen kada ora

- ¿Cuánto tarda?
  kwanto tarda

– Seis horas.
  says oras

- Dos boletos, for favor.
  dos boletos por fabor

Q How frequent are the coaches for Acapulco?
   How long does the trip take?

using the underground

you may say ...

Where is the nearest underground station?	¿Dónde está la estación de metro† más cercana?	*dondeh esta la estasyon deh metro mas serkana*
A ticket, please.	Un boleto, por favor.	*oon boleto por fabor*
Does this train go to Bellas Artes?	¿Este tren va a Bellas Artes?	*esteh tren ba a beyas artes*
What line is Capitolio on?	¿En qué línea está Capitolio?	*en keh leenea esta kapeetolyo*
Where do I change for Parque del Este?	¿Dónde cambio para Parque del Este?	*dondeh kambyo para parkeh del esteh*
Is the next station Independencia?	¿La próxima estación es Independencia?	*la prokseema estasyon es eendependensya*

you may hear ...

en la línea dos	*en la leenea dos*	on line 2
Tome la línea dos (dirección Tasqueña).	*tomeh la leenea dos (deereksyon taskenya)*	Take line 2 (towards Tasqueña).
Cambie en Plaza Venezuela.	*kambye en plasa beneswela*	Change at Plaza Venezuela.

taking the bus

you may say ...

Is there a bus stop (near here)?	¿Hay una parada de autobuses por aquí?	*iy oona parada deh owtobooses por akee*
Where can I take a bus?	¿Dónde puedo tomar un autobús?	*dondeh pwedo tomar oon owtoboos*
Do you go past Callao?	¿Pasa por Callao?	*pasa por kayao*
Is it far?	¿Está lejos?	*esta lehhos*
Can you tell me where to get off?	¿Me puede decir dónde bajarme?	*meh pwedeh deseer dondeh bahharmeh*

Getting **Around**

you may hear ...

A media hora, más o menos.	*a medya ora mas o menos*	About half an hour.
Aquí es.	*akee es*	It's here.

catching a taxi

you may say ...

Is there a taxi rank?	¿Hay un sitio de taxis?	*iy oon **see**tyo deh **tak**sees*

To the ... please.
  airport
  cathedral
	... por favor.
	  Al aeropuerto
	  A la catedral
		*por fa**bor**
		  al aero**pwer**to
		  a la kate**dral**

How much is it ...
  to the San Angel restaurant?
  to the Hotel Intercontinental?
	¿Cuánto es ...
	  al restaurante San Angel?
	  al Hotel Intercontinental?
		***kwan**to es*
		  *al restow**ran**teh san **an**hel*
		  *al o**tel** een*ter-*konteenen**tal***

Keep the change.	Quédese con el cambio.	*ke**deseh kon el **kam**byo*
Could I have a receipt?	¿Me puede dar un recibo?	*meh **pwe**deh dar oon re**see**bo*

sound check

In Spanish, the vowels always represent the same sound. Even in diphthongs – when two vowels occur together in one syllable – they keep their original individual sounds.

bueno *bweno*   gracias *grasyas*   tienda *tyenda*

h is always silent ... except in the combination **ch**
hay *iy*   hola *ola*   chocolate *tchokolateh*

Practise with these words:
hora *ora*   tiene *tyeneh*   vuelta *bwelta*   anoche *anotcheh*

try it out

find the right place
What is the Spanish word for the place where you would:

1 change money?
2 check your email?
3 catch a train?
4 withdraw some cash?
5 get information on tourist attractions?
6 take a local bus?
7 get petrol?

mix and match

Match the questions and answers.

1 ¿Perdone, hay un banco por aquí?
2 ¿Dónde está la estación de trenes, por favor?
3 ¿Cuánto cuesta?
4 ¿Cuánto tarda?
5 Quisiera alquilar un coche.

a Seis o siete horas.
b Cuatrocientos pesos al día.
c ¿Por cuánto tiempo?
d Allá en la esquina.
e Sí, hay dos o tres al final de la calle.

as if you were there

You stop a minibus. Follow the prompts to play your part.

(Ask if it goes past Bellas Artes)
Sí, justo enfrente.
(Ask how much it is to Bellas Artes)
Diez pesos por persona.
(You hand the driver the money and ask him to tell you where to get off)
Sí, no está lejos.
(later)
Aquí es. *(pointing)* Allí está Bellas Artes.
(Thank him)

linkup

¿Dónde está la plaza mayor?	**Where's** the main square?
¿Está lejos?	**Is it** far?
¿Hay un museo por aquí?	**Is there** a museum near here?
¿Tiene un horario?	**Do you have** a timetable?
Quisiera alquilar un coche.	**I'd like** to hire a car.
¿A qué hora sale el autobús?	**What time** does the bus leave?

'the' and 'a' in Spanish

You've probably noticed that you say:

el banco (the bank) **but la** catedral (the cathedral)
un museo (a museum) **but una** iglesia (a church)

This is because in Spanish words for things are either masculine or feminine.

The word for 'the' is el for a singular masculine word and la for a singular feminine word.

The word for 'a' or 'an' is un for a masculine word and una for a feminine word.

For more on articles, see the Language Builder, p130. ······⟩

how to ask a question

Sometimes questions are easy, because they follow the same pattern as in English:
¿Dónde está el banco? Where is the bank?
¿Cuánto es esto? How much is this?

But sometimes the word order is different:

¿Está cerca el banco? Is the bank near?
¿A qué hora sale el autobús? What time does the bus leave?

Notice that Spanish has no equivalent of the English use of 'do' or 'does' in questions.

For more tips on questions and question words, see the Language Builder, p134. ······›

saying where things are

Two very useful expressions when you're travelling around Latin America:

Está lejos. It's a long way.
Está cerca. It's close.

When you're saying what it's near to or far from, use de:

Está cerca de la Plaza Mayor. It's close to the main square.

When you're saying how far in time or distance, use a:

Está a dos kilómetros. It's two kilometres away.
Está a diez minutos. It's ten minutes away.

Notice that the word for 'is' here is está, not es. Está is always used when referring to where something or someone is. Use están when talking about more than one thing or person:

El cajero está en el segundo piso. The cash machine is on the second floor.
Los baños están junto a la entrada. The toilets are by the entrance.

For more on estar, see the Language Builder, p134. ······›

Somewhere **to Stay**

finding somewhere

The internet is a great place to look for accommodation in advance. Once you're there, notice boards and visitor's books in places frequented by tourists are a good source of information. Book ahead if you're planning to stay during public holidays.

types of accommodation

Hotels can be found in most of the large cities. They offer extensive leisure and business facilities, restaurants and bars. Credit cards are usually accepted and foreign currency changed.

Boutique hotels, at the top end of the scale, tend to be situated in scenic locations, upmarket seaside resorts and quiet colonial towns.

Hosterías and haciendas are converted land holdings and are often lovely examples of South American architecture.

Posadas, hospedajes, albergues, residencias, refugios and pensiones are categories of inexpensive accommodation of a broadly similar standard across Latin America; pensiones and residencias are officially the most basic of all.

Eco-lodges are becoming increasingly popular and offer holiday packages including full board and outdoor activities in areas of natural beauty and private reserves.

Estancias provide the opportunity to experience working cattle ranches and can be found in Uruguay, Chile and Argentina.

Backpacker/youth hostels (albergues juveniles/albergues de la juventud) are mainly found in Mexico, Costa Rica, Argentina, Uruguay and Chile. These often have luggage storage and kitchen facilities.

Casas particulares Visitors to Cuba are often able to stay in rooms or apartments let in private houses. Outside Havana, these are often very simple. Breakfast is included and other meals can be arranged.

Camping Although camping is not popular in most countries, it is becoming more common in southern and central Latin America. Most official sites are well equipped with hot, running water, toilets and fire pits.

rates

Most countries have some form of price regulation and there's sometimes a hotel tax and/or 10% service charge. Always check whether these are included in the price you are quoted. The good news is that foreigners do not always have to pay VAT.

children & people with disabilities

Check beforehand that your accommodation offers facilities for children; cots and high chairs are not always available. Big hotels in major cities that are on the tourist trail are much more likely to have facilities that cater for families with children and travellers with mobility problems than more remote destinations.

phrasemaker

finding a place
you may say ...

Is there a ... near here?	¿Hay ... por aquí?	iy ... por akee
hotel	un hotel	oon otel
hostel	un hostal	oon ostal
campsite	un camping	oon kampeen
Do you have a ... room?	¿Tienen ... una habitación† libre?	tyenen oona abeetasyon leebreh
flat to let?	un departamento/ apartamento para rentar?	oon departamento/ apartamento para rentar
a single/double room	una habitación individual/doble	oona abeetasyon eendeebeedwal/ dobleh
for ...	para ...	para
two nights	dos noches	dos notches
a weekend	un fin de semana	oon feen deh semana
a week	una semana	oona semana
two adults and a child	dos adultos y un niño	dos adooltos ee oon neenyo
three people	tres personas	tres personas
Can I see the room?	¿Puedo ver la habitación?	pwedo ber la abeetasyon
How much is the room?	¿Cuánto cuesta la habitación?	kwanto kwesta la abeetasyon
Is there a ...	¿Hay ...	iy
reduction for children?	descuento para niños?	deskwento para neenyos
single supplement?	recargo por un solo ocupante?	rekargo por oon solo okoopanteh
Do you have anything cheaper?	¿Tiene algo más barato?	tyeneh algo mas barato
It's fine.	Está bien.	esta byen

you may hear ...

¿Para cuántas noches/personas?	*para kwantas notches/ personas*	For how many nights/people?
Está todo lleno.	*esta todo yeno*	We're full.
El impuesto ... está incluido. es aparte.	*el eempwesto esta eenklooeedo es aparteh*	Tax is ... included. extra.
Los niños pagan la mitad.	*los neenyos pagan la meetath*	Children are half price.

check out 1

You ask about rooms in a hotel.

- Buenas tardes.
  bwenas tardes

○ Buenas tardes. ¿Tienen una habitación libre?
  bwenas tardes. tyenen oona abeetasyon leebreh

- ¿Individual o doble?
  eendeebeedwal o dobleh

○ Doble.
  dobleh

- Sí tenemos. ¿Para cuántas noches?
  see tenemos. para kwantas notches

○ Una noche.
  oona notcheh

- Muy bien.
  mwee byen

○ ¿Cuánto cuesta?
  kwanto kwesta

- Cuatrocientos pesos.
  kwatrosyentos pesos

Q How many nights are you staying?
How much is your double room?

facilities
you may say ...

Does it have ...	¿Tiene...	*tyeneh*
a bathroom?	baño?	*banyo*
a shower?	ducha†?	*dootcha*
a sea view?	vista al mar?	*beesta al mar*
a sink?	lavamanos?	*laba-manos*
WiFi?	modem/internet inalámbrico?	*modem/eenternet eenalambreeko*
a safe?	caja fuerte/caja de seguridad?	*kahha fwerteh/deh segooreedath*
with a ... bed	con cama ...	*kon kama*
double	doble/ matrimonial	*dobleh/ matreemonyal*
single	sencilla	*senseeya*
with ...	con ...	*kon*
twin beds	dos camas	*dos kamas*
air conditioning	aire acondicionado	*iyreh akondeesyonado*
a toilet	baño/excusado	*banyo/eskoosado*
Is breakfast included?	¿Está incluido el desayuno?	*esta eenklweedo el desayoono*
How much is ...	¿Cuánto cuesta ...	*kwanto kwesta*
full board?	con comidas?	*kon komeedas*
an extra bed?	una cama extra?	*oona kama estra*
How much is it without meals?	¿Cuánto cuesta sin comidas?	*kwanto kwesta seen komeedas*
We need a cot.	Necesitamos una cuna.	*neseseetamos oona koona*
Do you have a room on the ground floor?	¿Tienen un cuarto en el primer piso?	*tyenen oon kwarto en el preemer peeso*

Is the bathroom wheelchair-friendly?	¿Tiene baño adaptado para personas en silla de ruedas?	*tyeneh banyo adaptado para personas en seeya deh rwedas*

you may hear ...

El desayuno es aparte.	*el desayoono es aparteh*	Breakfast is extra.
Todo está incluido.	*todo esta eenklweedo*	Everything is included.
No incluye comidas.	*no eenklooyeh komeedas*	Meals are not included.
No tenemos camas matrimoniales.	*no tenemos kamas matreemonyales*	We don't have any double beds.

check out 2
You ask what is available in your double room.

○ ¿Hay aire acondicionado en las habitaciones?
iy iyreh akondeesyonado en las abeetasyones

– Sí, claro. Todas las habitaciones tienen aire acondicionado.
see klaro. todos las abeetasyones tyenen iyreh akondeesyonado

○ Bien. Son habitaciones dobles, ¿verdad?
byen. son abeetasyones dobles berdath

– Sí, todas son dobles con camas individuales.
see. todas son dobles kon kamas eendeebeedwales

○ ¿No tiene con cama matrimonial?
no tyeneh kon kama matreemonyal

– No, sólo con dos camas.
no solo kon dos kamas   (sólo = only)

○ Bueno, está bien.
bweno esta byen   (verdad = true/right)

Q You get air conditioning: true/false?
You'll be sleeping in a double bed: true/false?

45

checking in

you may say ...

I have a reservation.	Tengo una reservación/una reserva.	*tengo oona reserbasyon/oona reserba*
In the name of ...	A nombre de ...	*a nombreh deh*
What floor is it on?	¿En qué piso está?	*en keh peeso esta*
Where's the ... lift? staircase? dining room? garden?	¿Dónde está ... el ascensor†? la escalera? el comedor? el jardín?	*dondeh esta el asensor la eskalera el komedor el hhardeen*
What time is ... breakfast? dinner?	¿A qué hora es ... el desayuno? la cena?	*a keh ora es el desayoono la sena*
Is there ... internet access? a laundry service?	¿Hay ... internet? servicio de lavandería?	*iy eenternet serbeesyo deh labandereea*
Where can I ... park? ring abroad? get a taxi? leave my bags?	¿Dónde puedo ... estacionar†? llamar de larga distancia? tomar un taxi? guardar mis maletas†?	*dondeh pwedo estasyonar yamar deh larga deestansya tomar oon taksy gwardar mees maletas*

you may hear ...

Su nombre/pasaporte, por favor.	*soo nombreh/pasaporteh por fabor*	Your name/passport, please.
¿Quiere llenar este formulario?	*kyereh yenar esteh formoolaryo*	Please fill in this form.
(Es) la habitación número ...	*(es) la abeetasyon noomero*	(It's) room number ... (see p14 for numbers)

Somewhere **to Stay**

Está ...	*esta*	It's ...
en el tercer piso.	*en el terser peeso*	on the third floor.
a mano izquierda.	*a mano eeskyerda*	on the left.
a mano derecha.	*a mano deretcha*	on the right.
de (las) siete a (las) diez y media	*deh (las) syeteh a (las) dyes ee medya*	from seven to half past ten (see p13 for time)
Tenemos estacionamiento.	*tenemos estasyonamyento*	We have got a car park.
¿Cuál es su número de placa†?	*kwal es soo noomero deh plaka*	Your registration number?
¿Van a cenar?	*ban a senar*	Are you going to have dinner?
Aquí está la llave.	*akee esta la yabeh*	Here's the key.

asking for help

you may say ...

Could I have an alarm call at eight?	¿Me puede despertar a las ocho?	*meh pwedeh despertar a las otcho*
Could you get me a taxi?	¿Me puede conseguir un taxi?	*meh pwedeh konsegeer oon taksy*
Do you have ...	¿Tiene ...	*tyeneh*
an extra key?	una llave adicional?	*oona yabeh adeesyonal*
a pen?	un bolígrafo?	*oon boleegrafo*
My room hasn't been made up.	No me han limpiado el cuarto.	*no meh an leempyado el kwarto*
Can I have ...	¿Me puede dar ... por favor?	*meh pwede dar ... por fabor*
another pillow?	otra almohada	*otra almwada*
another towel?	otra toalla	*otra twaya*
another glass?	otro vaso	*otro baso*
There isn't any ...	No hay ...	*no iy*
hot water.	agua caliente.	*agwa kalyenteh*
soap.	jabón.	*hhabon*
toilet paper.	papel higiénico.	*papel eehhyeneeko*
There aren't any ...	No hay ...	*no iy*
blankets.	cobijas†.	*kobeehhas*
hangers.	ganchos†.	*gantchos*

How do you work the ...	¿Cómo funciona ...	*komo foonsyona*
fan?	el ventilador?	*el benteelador*
telephone?	el teléfono?	*el telefono*
blind?	la persiana?	*la persyana*
The ... isn't working.	... no funciona.	*... no foonsyona*
tap	La llave del agua†	*la yabeh del agwa*
lock	La cerradura	*la serradoora*
light	La luz	*la loos*
The room is very noisy.	Entra mucho ruido en mi cuarto.	*entra mootcho rweedo en mee kwarto*
The room is very hot/cold.	En el cuarto hace mucho calor/frío.	*en el kwarto aseh mootcho kalor/freeo*
Do you have ...	¿Tiene ...	*tyeneh*
an iron?	una plancha?	*oona plantcha*
a hairdryer?	un secador de pelo?	*oon sekador deh pelo*
a mobile phone charger?	un cargador de celular?	*oon kargador deh seloolar*
a current adapter?	un adaptador de corriente?	*oon adaptador deh korryenteh*

you may hear ...

Ahora/Ahorita le mando a alguien.	*aora/aoreeta leh mando a algyen*	I'll send someone up straight away.
Le mando ...	*leh mando*	I'll send you ...
uno/una.	*oon/oona*	one.
unos/unas.	*oonos/oonas*	some.

checking out
you may say ...

I'd like to pay the bill.	Quisiera pagar la cuenta.	*keesyera pagar la kwenta*
by credit/debit card	con tarjeta de crédito/débito	*kon tarhheta deh kredeeto/debeeto*
with traveller's cheques	con cheques de viajero	*kon tchekes deh byahhero*

| with cash | en efectivo | *en efekteebo* |
| I think there's a mistake. | Creo que hay un error. | *kreo keh iy oon error* |

you may hear ...

¿Qué habitación?	*keh abeetasyon*	Which room?
La llave, por favor.	*la yabeh, por fabor*	Your key, please.
¿Cómo va a pagar?	*komo ba a pagar*	How are you going to pay?
¿Quiere firmar aquí?	*qyereh feermar akee*	Sign here, please.
Aquí tiene su recibo.	*akee tyeneh soo reseebo*	Here's your receipt.

check out 3

You check out and pay the bill.

○ Quisiera pagar la cuenta.
keesyera pagar la kwenta

– Sí, señor. ¿Qué habitación?
see senyor. keh abeetasyon

○ Ochenta y nueve. ¿Cuánto es?
otchenta ee nwebeh. kwanto es

– Cuatrocientos sesenta y siete pesos, todo incluido.
¿Cómo va a pagar?
kwatrosyentos sesenta ee syeteh pesos, todo eenklweedo. komo ba a pagar

○ Con tarjeta de crédito.
kon tarhheta deh kredeeto

– Muy bien ... ¿Quiere firmar aquí? ... Gracias. Aquí tiene su recibo. Adiós y buen viaje.
mwee byen ... kyereh feermar akee ... grasyas. akee tyeneh soo reseebo. adyos ee bwen byahheh

Q You pay less than five hundred pesos: true/false?
You got a receipt: true/false?

at the campsite

you may say ...

Do you have a space for a tent/caravan?	¿Tiene lugar para una tienda†/un trailer?	*tyeneh loogar para oona tyenda/oon triyler*
How much is it per ...	¿Cuánto cuesta por ...	*kwanto kwesta por*
person?	persona?	*persona*
tent?	tienda?	*tyenda*
Is there...	¿Hay ...	*iy*
a shop?	tienda†?	*tyenda*
a laundry?	lavandería?	*labandereea*
a swimming pool?	piscina†?	*peeseena*
Where are the ...	¿Dónde están ...	*dondeh estan*
showers?	las duchas?	*las dootchas*
the dustbins?	los basureros?	*los basooreros*
the toilets?	los baños?	*los banyos*

you may hear ...

Cuesta ... pesos por ...	*kwesta ... pesos por*	It costs ... pesos per ...
persona.	*persona*	person.
coche.	*kotcheh*	car.
tienda.	*tyenda*	tent.

sound check

Spanish word-stress patterns are very consistent and follow two rules:

In words ending in a vowel or **n** or **s**, the stress falls on the last syllable but one:

amigo   *ameego*   buenas   ***bwe**nas*   tienen   ***tye**nen*

In words ending in a consonant other than **n** or **s**, the stress falls on the last syllable:

hotel   *o**tel***   comer   *ko**mer***   ¡Salud!   *sa**looth***

When these rules are broken, the word has an acute accent ´; the stress then falls on the accented syllable, whatever the ending. The accent does not change the sound quality of the vowel where it falls.

número   ***noo**mero*   menú   *me**noo***   pensión   *pen**syon***

Practise these words:

ducha   ***doo**tcha*   ascensor   *asen**sor***   teléfono   *te**le**fono*

try it out

'a' puzzle
Only the letter **a** remains in these words. Use the definitions to complete them.

1   _ a _ _ _ a _ _ _ _   (a place to sleep)
2   _ _ a _ _   (necessary to get into your room)
3   a _ _ _ _ _ _ _   (an easy way to get to the top floor)
4   _ a _ _   (may be en-suite or shared)
5   _ _ _ a _ _ _ _   (the first meal of the day)

as if you were there

Imagine you're in your hotel room and you pick up the phone. Make your complaint according to the prompts.

Recepción, buenas noches.
(Complain that there's no soap)
¿Qué habitación?
(Tell the receptionist your room number is 26 and ask how the shower works)
Ahorita le mando a alguien.

linkup

¿Tienen un lugar para tienda?	**Do you have** a space for a tent?
¿Dónde está la piscina?	**Where's** the swimming pool?
¿Dónde están las duchas?	**Where are** the showers?
¿Hay internet?	**Is there** internet access?
No hay ventilador.	**There isn't** a fan.
La ducha **no funciona.**	The shower **doesn't work.**

describing things

When you say 'The hotel is very cheap' in Spanish, the words go in the same order as in English:

El hotel es muy barato. **The hotel is very cheap.**

But if you say 'a cheap hotel', the word order changes:

un hotel barato a cheap hotel

One or two exceptions are:

el primer piso the first floor
el segundo plato the second course

The words barato, doble, individual are known as adjectives or describing words.

Many adjectives in Spanish end in −o or −a. These adjectives change according to the gender of the word they describe:

un hotel modern**o** a modern hotel (hotel is masculine, so you use the masculine form moderno).
una cama cómod**a** a comfortable bed (cama is feminine, so cómoda has its feminine ending −a').

Adjectives ending in −e are the same for both masculine and feminine words:

un hotel grande
una habitación grande

For more on adjectives, see the Language Builder, p131. ┈┈⟩

saying 'no': negatives

The word no means 'no':

¿Tienen una habitación individual? No, lo siento.
Do you have a single room? No, I'm sorry.

but it also means 'not', 'isn't' or 'doesn't':

No hay aire acondicionado. There isn't any air conditioning.
El ascensor no funciona. The lift doesn't work.

Buying **Things**

opening hours

Shop and business opening hours vary from country to country, but are generally from 9.30 or 10am to 5 or 6pm). Many places, especially in smaller cities or towns, may close during the early afternoon (midday to 2 or 3pm). Expect most to be closed on Saturday afternoon and all day on Sunday. Supermarkets usually don't close for lunch and some in large urban centres are 24-hour. Upmarket western-style shopping centres will be open long hours and at the weekend.

markets

If you are looking to buy **artesanías** (handicrafts), you are in the right place! Latin American crafts include a variety of beautiful and colourful souvenirs that can be found at **ferias artesanales** (craft markets). In small towns, these will be found on or near the main square. Prices are usually very reasonable, but bargaining is common practice.

Latin American countries are famous for their indigenous food markets. It's easy to find markets open daily where you can buy fresh local farm produce, speciality foods, liqueurs and groceries. In the Andean region in particular, you can find wonderful exotic fruits, high-quality fish and seafood, and countless varieties of corn and potatoes.

Street and flea markets are a great way to have a fun day outside, combining shopping and live entertainment. These usually come to life every weekend, with hundreds of people gathering to buy and sell everything from inexpensive trinkets to pricey antiques. Mexico, Argentina and Chile have some of the largest, with numerous booths and eateries, and entertaining street performers who create an atmosphere of festivity.

shopping centres

Large shopping centres in major cities look remarkably western in style. It's not uncommon to find branches of large retail chains and the best national and international brands. As you may expect, the variety on offer usually comes at a price. Outdoor and sports gear or camping equipment are harder to come by in non-specialised shops, so make sure you bring everything you need from home.

buying essentials

Supermarkets are well stocked in just about all of the essential day-to-day goods that you may need to replenish while travelling. You'll have no difficulty buying things like tampons, condoms, contact lens supplies and general toiletries. If you are travelling to remote areas, it's worth stocking up in city supermarkets before setting out.

Chemists sell a wide range of over-the-counter medicines, but toiletries, photographic supplies and cosmetics can be harder to find unless you are in a large urban centre.

phrasemaker

general phrases

you may say ...

Do you have any ...	¿Tiene ...	*tyeneh*
milk?	leche?	*letcheh*
oil?	aceite?	*asayteh*
matches?	fósforos/cerillas?	*fosforos/sereeyas*
How much is it/are they?	¿Cuánto cuesta/cuestan?	*kwanto kwesta/kwestan*
How much are ...	¿Cuánto cuestan ...	*kwanto kwestan*
the bananas?	los plátanos†?	*los platanos*
the plums?	las ciruelas?	*las seerwelas*
this (one)	éste/ésta*	*esteh/esta*
these (ones)	éstos/éstas	*estos/estas*
that (one)	ése/ésa	*eseh/esa*
those (ones)	ésos/ésas	*esos/esas*
I'm just looking.	Sólo estoy mirando.	*solo estoy meerando*
How much is it (altogether)?	¿Cuánto es (todo)?	*kwanto es (todo)*
Nothing else, thanks.	Nada más, gracias.	*nada mas grasyas*
It's very nice.	Es muy bonito/a.	*es mwee boneeto/a*
They're very expensive.	Son muy caros/as.	*son mwee karos/as*
Is that your best price?	¿Es el último precio?	*es el oolteemo presyo*
I'll give you 50 pesos.	Le doy cincuenta pesos.	*leh doy seenkwenta pesos*
Do you have anything cheaper?	¿Tiene algo más barato?	*tyeneh algo mas barato*

you may hear ...

¿En qué puedo servirle?	*en keh pwedo serbeerleh*	Can I help you?
¿Qué desea?	*keh desea*	What would you like?

Buying **Things**

¿Le gusta/gustan?	*leh **goos**ta/**goos**tan*	Do you like it/them?
Claro que sí.	*kla**ro keh see***	Of course.
¿Algo más?	*al**go mas***	Anything else?
Perdone, no tenemos.	*per**do**neh no te**ne**mos*	I'm sorry, we don't have any.
Sólo tengo ...	*so**lo **ten**go*	I only have ...
No tengo ...	*no **ten**go*	I don't have ...
Aquí tiene.	*a**kee tye**neh*	Here you are.
Son quinientos cuarenta pesos.	*son kee**nyen**tos kwa**ren**ta **pe**sos*	That's 540 pesos.
Es precio fijo.	*es **pre**syo **fee**hho*	The price is fixed.

(*For more about masculine, feminine and plural word endings, see the Language Builder, p130.)

shops

baker's	la panadería	*la panade**ree**a*
bookshop	la librería	*la leebre**ree**a*
butcher's	la carnicería	*la karneese**ree**a*
cake shop	la pastelería	*la pastele**ree**a*
department store	el almacén por departamentos	*el alma**sen** por departa**men**tos*
fruit shop	la frutería	*la froote**ree**a*
greengrocer's	la verdulería	*la berdoole**ree**a*
hairdresser's/ barber's	la peluquería/la barbería	*la pelooke**ree**a/la barbe**ree**a*
handicraft shop	la tienda de artesanías†	*la **tyen**da deh artesa**nee**as*
jeweller's	la joyería	*la hhoye**ree**a*
newspaper stand	el puesto de periódicos†	*el **pwes**to deh peryo**dee**kos*
post office	el correo	*el ko**rre**o*
shoe shop	la zapatería	*la sapate**ree**a*
super(market)	el (super)mercado	*el (**soo**per)mer**ka**do*
tobacconist's	la tabaquería/ cigarrería	*la tabake**ree**a/ seegarre**ree**a*

quantities

you may say ...

I'll have ... please.	¿Me puede dar ... por favor?	meh *pwedeh* dar ... por fa*bor*
two kilos	dos kilos	dos *kee*los
100 grammes	cien gramos	syen *gramos*
I'll have a quarter of a kilo of ...	¿Me puede dar un cuarto de kilo de ...	meh *pwedeh* dar oon *kwarto* deh *keelo* deh
ham.	jamón?	hha*mon*
cheese.	queso?	*keso*
I'd like ...	Quisiera ...	kee*syera*
a box of	una caja de	*oona kahha* deh
a tin of	una lata de	*oona lata* deh
a loaf of bread	una barra de pan	*oona barra* deh pan
a jar of (coffee)	un frasco de (café)	oon *frasko* deh (ka*feh*)
a packet of (butter)	un paquete de (mantequilla†)	oon pa*keteh* deh (mante*keeya*)
a bottle of (mineral water)	una botella de (agua mineral)	*oona* bo*teya* deh (*agwa* meene*ral*)
a litre/kilo	un litro/kilo	oon *leetro*/*keelo*
half a litre/kilo	medio litro/kilo	*medyo leetro*/*keelo*
a dozen (eggs)	una docena (de huevos)	*oona* do*sena* (deh) *webos*
a little bit of ...	un poquito de ...	oon po*keeto* deh
Can I have ...	¿Me puede dar ...	meh *pwedeh* dar
another?	otro/otra?	*otro*/*otra*
a bit more/less?	un poquito más/menos?	oon po*keeto* mas/*menos*
a bag?	una bolsa?	*oona bolsa*

you may hear ...

| ¿Cuánto/cuánta quiere? | *kwanto*/*kwanta kyereh* | How much would you like? |
| ¿Cuántos/cuántas quiere? | *kwantos*/*kwantas kyereh* | How many would you like? |

fruit & vegetables

apple	la manzana	*la man**sa**na*
avocado	el aguacate†	*el agwa**ka**teh*
beans	los frijoles/los porotos†	*los free**hho**les/los po**ro**tos*
carrot	la zanahoria	*la sana**o**rya*
coconut	el coco	*el **ko**ko*
grapes	las uvas	*las **oo**bas*
lettuce	la lechuga	*la le**tchoo**ga*
lime/lemon	el limón	*el lee**mon***
mango	el mango	*el **man**go*
melon	el melón	*el me**lon***
mushrooms	los champiñones/los hongos	*los tchampee**nyo**nes/los **on**gos*
olives	las aceitunas	*las asay**too**nas*
onion	la cebolla	*la se**bo**ya*
orange	la naranja	*la na**ran**hha*
papaya	la papaya†	*la pa**pa**ya*
peach	el durazno/el melocotón	*el doo**ras**no/el meloko**ton***
pear	la pera	*la **pe**ra*
pepper	el pimiento†	*el pee**myen**to*
pineapple	la piña†	*la **pee**nya*
potato	la papa	*la **pa**pa*
strawberry	la fresa†	*la **fre**sa*
tomato	el tomate†	*el to**ma**teh*
watermelon	la sandía/la patilla	*la san**dee**a/la pa**tee**ya*

check out 1

You're at the market buying some fruit.

○ Buenos días. ¿Tiene mangos?
bwenos deeas. tyeneh mangos

- Perdone, no tenemos.
perdoneh no tenemos

○ ¿Cuánto cuestan las naranjas?
kwanto kwestan las naranhhas

- Doce pesos el kilo.
doseh pesos el keelo

○ Me puede dar dos kilos, y una papaya?
meh pwedeh dar dos keelos y oona papaya

- ¿Algo más?
algo mas

○ No, gracias. ¿Cuánto es?
no grasyas. kwanto es

Q Why didn't you get mangoes?
How much did you pay for the oranges?

buying handicrafts

you may say ...

Where can I buy ...	¿Dónde puedo comprar ...	*dondeh pwedo komprar*
handicrafts?	artesanías?	*artesaneeas*
jewellery	joyas?	*hhoyas*
What is it made of?	¿De qué está hecho/a?	*deh keh esta etcho/a*
What are they made of?	¿De qué están hechos/as?	*deh keh estan etchos/as*
a (wool) rug	un tapete/una alfombra (de lana)	*oon tapeteh/oona alfombra (deh lana)*

| a hammock | una hamaca | *oona amaka* |
| a (pottery) vase | un jarrón (de barro) | *oon hharron (deh barro)* |

you may hear ...

Es hecho/a a mano.	*es etcho/a a mano*	It's handmade.
Son hechos/as a mano.	*son etchos/as a mano*	They're handmade.
Está hecho/a de ...	*esta etcho/a deh*	It's made of ...
madera.	*madera*	wood.
cuero/piel.	*kwero/pyel*	leather.
Están hechos/as de ...	*estan etchos/as deh*	They're made of ...
plata.	*plata*	silver.
oro.	*oro*	gold.

shopping for clothes & shoes

you may say ...

I'd like ...	Quisiera ...	*keesyera*
a sweater.	un suéter.	*oon sweter*
some boots.	unas botas.	*oonas botas*
some sandals.	unas sandalias†	*oonas sandalyas*
size (clothes/shoes)	talla/número	*taya/noomero*
Can I try it on?	¿Puedo probármelo/la?	*pwedo probarmelo/la*
Can I try them on?	¿Puedo probármelos/las?	*pwedo probarmelos/las*

Where are the fitting rooms?	¿Dónde están los probadores?	*dondeh estan los probadores*
It's a bit ...	Está algo ...	*esta algo*
big.	grande.	*grandeh*
small.	chico/a/pequeño/a.	*tcheeko/a/pekenyo/a*
They're a bit ...	Están algo ...	*estan algo*
big.	grandes.	*grandes*
small.	chicos/as.	*tcheekos/as*
Do you have the same in ...	¿Tiene lo mismo en ...	*tyeneh lo meesmo en*
size 42?	talla cuarenta y dos?	*taya kwarenta ee dos*
medium?	mediano?	*medyano*
Do you have one in silk/blue?	¿Tiene uno/una en seda/azul?	*tyeneh oono/oona en seda/asool*
Do you have any in green/cotton?	¿Tiene unos/unas en verde/algodón?	*tyeneh oonos/oonas en berdeh/algodon*
I like it/them.	Me gusta/gustan.	*meh goosta/goostan*
I'll take it.	Me lo/la llevo.	*meh lo/la yebo*
I'll take them.	Me los/las llevo.	*meh los/las yebo*
I'll leave it.	No me lo/la llevo.	*no meh lo/la yebo*
Do you take credit cards?	¿Se aceptan tarjetas de crédito?	*seh aseptan tarhhetas deh kredeeto*

you may hear ...

| Le queda/quedan bien. | *leh keda/kedan byen* | It/they suit(s) you. |
| No, solamente efectivo. | *no solamenteh efekteebo* | No, cash only. |

clothes & accessories

belt	el cinturón	*el seentooron*
blouse	la blusa	*la bloosa*
bracelet	la pulsera	*la poolsera*
coat	el abrigo†	*el abreego*
dress	el vestido	*el besteedo*

earrings	los aretes†	*los aretes*
gloves	los guantes	*los gwantes*
hat	el sombrero	*el sombrero*
jacket (casual)	la chaqueta†	*la tchaketa*
jacket (formal)	el saco	*el sako*
jeans	los jeans	*los yeens*
knickers	las pantaletas/los pantis†	*las pantaletas/los pantees*
necklace	el collar	*el koyar*
ring	el anillo	*el aneeyo*
scarf	la bufanda	*la boofanda*

check out 2

You try your hand at bargaining.

- ○ ¿Qué desea?
  keh desea

- ¿Cuánto cuesta este anillo?
  kwanto kwesta esteh aneeyo

- ○ Cien pesos.
  syen pesos

- Le doy setenta pesos.
  leh doy setenta pesos

- ○ Perdone, es el último precio.
  perdoneh es el oolteemo presyo

- ¿Tiene algo más barato?
  tyeneh algo mas barato

- ○ Sí, estos aretes cuestan sesenta y nueve.
  see estos aretes kwestan sesenta ee nwebeh

- Bueno, me los llevo.
  bweno meh los yebo

Q How much is the ring?
What do you decide to buy?

shirt	la camisa	*la kameesa*
shoes	los zapatos	*los sapatos*
shorts	los shorts	*los tchorts*
skirt	la falda†	*la falda*
suit	el traje	*el trahheh*
swimming costume	el traje de baño†	*el trahheh deh banyo*
tie	la corbata	*la korbata*
trainers	los tenis/las zapatillas	*los tenees/las sapateeyas*
trousers	los pantalones	*los pantalones*
T-shirt	la camiseta/la playera†	*la kameeseta/la playera*
underpants	los calzoncillos	*los kalsonseeyos*

at the newspaper stand

you may say …

Do you have any … newspapers?	¿Tiene periódicos† …	*tyeneh peryodeekos*
English	ingleses?	*eengleses*
foreign	extranjeros?	*estranhheros*
Do you have …	¿Tiene …	*tyeneh*
any magazines?	revistas?	*rebeestas*
a bus/tube guide?	una guía de autobuses/del metro?†	*oona geea deh owtobooses/del metro*
Do you sell international phone cards?	Tiene tarjetas de teléfono internacionales?	*tyeneh tarhhetas deh telefono eenternasyonales*

Buying **Things**

check out 3

You go to the *puesto de periódicos* thinking of home.

○ Buenas tardes, ¿tiene periódicos ingleses?
  bwenas tardes. tyeneh peryodeekos eengleses

- No, pero tengo The News. Es mexicano pero está en inglés.
  no pero tengo the news. es mehheekano pero esta en eengles

○ ¿Y revistas?
  ee rebeestas

- Tengo Newsweek y Time.
  tengo newsweek ee time

○ Me puede dar The News y Time?
  meh pwede dar the news ee time

Q Are there any English newspapers?

at the post office

you may say ...

How much is a stamp for Europe?	¿Cuánto vale una estampilla para Europa?	*kwanto baleh oona estampeeya para eooropa*

for a ...
   letter
   postcard
	para ...
	   una carta
	   una (tarjeta) postal
		para
		   oona karta
		   oona (tarhheta) postal

Two stamps, please.	Dos estampillas, por favor.	*dos estampeeyas por fabor*
I'd like to send this to England.	Quisiera mandar esto a Inglaterra.	*keesyera mandar esto a eenglaterra*

Standard or registered mail?	¿Correo normal o certificado?	korreo normal o serteefeekado
Where is it going?	¿Adónde va?	adondeh ba
What does the parcel contain?	¿Qué contiene el paquete?	keh kontyeneh el paketeh
Does it contain any valuables?	¿Contiene algo de valor?	contyeneh algo deh balor

photography
you may say …

Can you develop this film, please?	¿Me puede revelar este rollo?	meh pwedeh rebelar esteh rroyo
Can you put them on a disc?	¿Puede grabarlas en un disco?	pwedeh grabarlas en oon deesko
When will it be ready?	¿Para cuándo está listo?	para kwando esta leesto
I'd like a (colour) film.	Quisiera un rollo (a colores).	keesyera oon rroyo (a kolores)
a disposable camera	una cámara desechable	oona kamara desetchableh
normal/large size	tamaño normal/ grande	tamanyo normal/ grandeh

you may hear …

¿Cuándo los/las quiere?	kwando los/las kyereh	When do you want them?
mañana por la mañana/tarde	manyana por la manyana/tardeh	tomorrow morning/ afternoon
en una hora/ veinticuatro horas	en oona ora/ benteekwatro oras	in one hour/24 hours
¿Mate o brillante?	mateh o breeyanteh	Matt or gloss?
¿Qué tamaño?	keh tamanyo	What size?
¿Cuántas copias de cada una?	kwantas kopyas deh kada oona	How many sets?

Buying **Things**

sound check

rr (double **r**) is always strongly rolled:

correo *ko*rre*o*   cigarrería *seegarrereea*   barra *ba*rra

The single **r** is also strongly rolled at the beginning of a word:

rollo *rroyo*   rápido *rrapeedo*   revista *rrebeesta*

but elsewhere is pronounced more lightly, more like the 'r' in 'rain':

grabar *grabar*   mandar *mandar*   para *para*

try it out

food mixer

Rearrange the syllables in these words to make things you can eat or drink.

mónja lónme bollace soque voshue janaran chele chulega

phrase matcher

Match each of the phrases (1–5) with the best reply (a–e).

1	¿Le gusta?	**a**	Grande.
2	¿Algo más?	**b**	Medio kilo.
3	¿Qué talla?	**c**	Sí, me lo llevo.
4	¿Cuánto quiere?	**d**	Doscientos treinta pesos.
5	¿Cuánto es?	**e**	No, nada más, gracias.

as if you were there.

You are buying souvenirs at a handicrafts shop

¿Le gusta el sombrero?
(Say you like it and ask how much it is)
Doscientos veinte pesos.
(Ask if they take credit cards)
No, solamente efectivo.
(Ask if it's her best price)
Sí, es precio fijo.
(Say you'll take it)

linkup

<table>
<tr><td rowspan="6" style="writing-mode: vertical-rl">key phrases</td><td>¿Tiene aceitunas?</td><td>Do you have any olives?</td></tr>
<tr><td>¿Me puede dar medio kilo?</td><td>Could I have half a kilo?</td></tr>
<tr><td>Me gusta este sombrero.</td><td>I like this hat.</td></tr>
<tr><td>¿Cuánto cuesta esta camisa?</td><td>How much is this shirt?</td></tr>
<tr><td>¿Cuánto cuestan estas botas?</td><td>How much are these boots?</td></tr>
<tr><td>¿Tiene uno más grande?</td><td>Do you have a bigger one?</td></tr>
</table>

asking about availability

There are two ways of asking about availability in Spanish, by using ¿Tiene ...? or ¿Hay ....?.

¿Tiene manzanas? Do you have any apples?
¿Hay manzanas? Are there any apples?
¿Hay leche? Is there any milk?

Buying **Things**

And the replies you are likely to hear are:

Sí, tengo/tenemos manzanas. Yes, I've/we've got (some) apples.
No, no tengo/tenemos manzanas. No, I/we don't have any apples.
Sí, hay manzanas. Yes, we have (some) apples.
No, no hay manzanas. No, we don't have any apples.

Notice that in Spanish you don't need the word for 'some' or 'any'.

Note also that the useful word hay means both 'Is there?' and 'Are there?' (as well as 'There is/There are').

comparing things

If you want something bigger, smaller or cheaper use más 'more':

Este sombrero es **más caro**. This hat is **more expensive**.
Quisiera algo **más barato**. I'd like something **cheaper** (literally, 'more cheap').
¿Tiene una mochila **más pequeña**? Do you have a **smaller** (literally, 'more small') rucksack?

more than one

To talk about more than one of something, just add –s to nouns or adjectives that end in **-o**, **-a** or **-e**:

Dos jugo**s** frío**s**. Two cold juices.
Un kilo de uva**s** negra**s**. A kilo of black grapes.
Los guante**s** verde**s**. The green gloves.

And add **-es** to nouns and adjectives that end in a consonant:

Quisiera cuatro melo**nes**. I'd like four melons.
Dos suéte**res** azu**les**. Two blue jumpers.

For more on the singular and plural, see the Language Builder, p130.

Café **Life**

what to drink

Mate The national beverage of Argentina, **yerba mate** is a tea, similar in appearance to green tea, that is considered to have health benefits. Drinking **mate** in groups is both a social ritual and a sign of friendship.

Wine Argentina and Chile have well-established wine-drinking cultures and their locally produced wines are excellent.

Tropical fruit juices Treat yourself to a healthy fresh-fruit blend of some of the most exotic fruits in the world. Available in most countries at food markets, juice bars and restaurants, **jugos de frutas** are delicious and plentiful. For a thicker, smoothie-like texture, try **batidos** or **licuados**, which are made with milk.

Coffee Surprisingly for a region that produces some of the finest blends, coffee is of remarkably poor quality in most places. In Colombia, a watered-down espresso is known as **tinto**. If your choice is latte (**café con leche**), ask for the coffee and milk separately, or you will get a very bland milky drink with sugar. To try export-quality Colombian coffee, try speciality cafés.

Tequila Although originally from Tequila, a town in western Mexico, this distilled alcoholic beverage, made primarily from the blue agave, is famous worldwide. Most common tequilas are 38% to 40% alcohol and production is tightly regulated to ensure the best quality.

speciality drinks

Aguardiente Distilled brandy from the Andean region, derived from fruits or sugar cane.

Aguas frescas Flavoured water. **Agua de Jamaica** (hibiscus flavour) and **agua de tamarindo** (tamarind flavour) are popular.

Guarapo A fermented sugar cane or fruit drink (mildly alcoholic), typical of the Andean region.

Café de olla Black coffee with raw cane sugar and cinnamon.

Chicha A strong drink from the Andean region, made from fermented fruit juices or maize.

Cuba libre Caribbean rum and coke.

Masato A fermented yucca or rice drink (sometimes mildly alcoholic), from Colombia and Peru.

Mezcal A Mexican distilled cactus juice; some kinds are bottled with a worm at the bottom.

Pisco (sour) A regional brandy made of grapes, lemon juice, egg white and regional bitters, from Peru and Chile.

Pulque Mexican fermented cactus juice.

Sangría A mixture of red wine, lemonade and pieces of fruit.

Tequila (y una sangrita) Tequila (with a tomato and orange chaser).

what to eat

Empanadas These pastries, filled with seafood, meat, cheese, vegetables or fruit, are popular throughout Latin America.

Tamales or **ayacas** This traditional dish varies from one country to another, but in general is a staple of cornmeal with pork, chicken or beef (or a mix of the three) and spices rolled out in corn husks or wrapped in banana leaves.

Arepas Corn cakes first made by the Indians of Colombia and Venezuela. Baked, grilled or fried, **arepas** come with a huge variety of fillings or toppings, both sweet and savoury.

places to go

Cafeterías (the generic name for a place where you can have a drink and a simple meal) are present in many guises, from outlets selling drinks and pastries to small restaurants serving savoury specialities.

Confiterías (coffee shops) or salones de té (tea rooms), found in the Southern Cone, are great places to have hot drinks, sandwiches and cakes, and to mingle with the locals. In some Argentinian confiterías you can even enjoy a tango show.

Bars vary hugely. Most major cities have an upmarket nightlife district where you can try local and imported beer and spirits at bargain prices, while soaking up the friendly atmosphere and enjoying the music and dancing. In some countries and in rural areas, bars can be less salubrious and should be avoided by unaccompanied women. Mexico's small cantinas are great places for cheap beer and pool.

Pulquería A Mexican shop or tavern selling pulque (a fermented drink made from the sap of the agave cactus).

Chichería Chicha, the sacred drink of the Incas, is still a very popular choice for many in rural Peru today. A visit to a traditional chichería, where you can taste the different varieties and see it made, is a must.

Cervecería A place where cerveza (beer) is brewed or sold. Aside from international brands, you can find good local bottled lager, although connoisseurs will be disappointed by the poor variety of draught beer and lack of ales and bitters.

Taquería These informal Mexican eateries specialising in tacos line the streets of Mexico's towns and cities.

Saltañería Shops selling Bolivia's delicious version of the empanada.

phrasemaker

asking what there is
you may say ...

Do you have any ...	¿Tiene ...	*tyeneh*
sandwiches/rolls?	sándwiches?	*sandweetches*
vegetarian food?	comida para	*komeeda para*
	vegetarianos?	*behhetaryanos*
What ... do you have?	¿Qué ... tiene?	*keh ... tyeneh*
beers	cervezas	*serbesas*
cold/hot drinks	bebidas frías/	*bebeedas freeas/*
	calientes	*kalyentes*
(bottled) soft drinks	refrescos†	*refreskos*
	(embotellados)	*(emboteyados)*
fresh juices	jugos naturales?	*hhoogos natoorales*

you may hear ...

Tenemos ...	*tenemos*	We have ...
No, no tenemos ...	*no no tenemos*	No, we don't have any ...
Sólo hay ...	*solo iy*	There's only ...
Hay jugos de ...	*iy hhoogos deh*	There's ... juice.

ordering
you may say ...

I'd like ...	Quisiera ...	*keesyera*
a hamburger.	una hamburguesa.	*oona amboorgesa*
a hot dog.	un perro caliente/	*oon perro kalyenteh/*
	un hot dog†.	*oon hhot dog*
some crisps/chips.	unas papas fritas.	*oonas papas freetas*
A portion of ...	Una porción de ... por	*oona porsyon deh ...*
please.	favor.	*por fabor*
olives	aceitunas	*asaytoonas*
peanuts	maní†	*manee*

Can I have a ... (corn) pastry?	¿Me puede dar una empanada de ...	*meh* **pwe***deh dar* **oo***na empana*da *deh*
ham	jamón?	*hha***mon**
chicken	pollo?	**po***yo*
Is it (very) spicy?	¿Pica (mucho)?	*pee*ka *(***moo***tcho)*
with ...	con ...	*kon*
everything	todo	**to***do*
cheese	queso	**ke***so*
without ...	sin ...	*seen*
onion	cebolla	*se***bo***ya*
chilli	chile/ají	*tchee*leh/a*hhee*
to take away	para llevar	*para ye***bar**
to eat in	para comer aquí	*para ko*mer a*kee*

you may hear ...

¿Qué desea?	*keh de***se***a*	What would you like?
¿Qué va a tomar?	*keh ba a to***mar**	What are you going to have?
¿Qué quiere de ...	*keh* **kye***reh deh*	What would you like to ...
beber?	be**ber**	drink?
comer?	ko**mer**	eat?
Sí, cómo no.	*see* **ko***mo no*	Yes, of course.
¿Es todo?	*es* **to***do*	Is that everything?
Sí, pica (un poco).	*see* **pee***ka (oon* **po***ko)*	Yes, it's (a bit) hot/spicy.
No, no pica.	*no no* **pee***ka*	No, it's not hot/spicy.

Café **Life**

check out 1

You buy sandwiches for a picnic.

○ ¿Qué sándwiches tienen?
keh sandweetches tyenen

- De pollo, de jamón y vegetariano.
deh poyo de hhamon ee behhetaryano

○ Me puede dar dos de jamón y dos de pollo, por favor.
meh pwedeh dar dos deh hhamon ee dos deh poyo por fabor

- ¿Con todo?
kon todo

○ Sin chile.
seen tcheeleh

Q What fillings are you offered?

soft drinks

iced tea	un té helado	*oon teh elado*
... juice	un jugo de ...	*oon hhoogo deh*
orange	naranja	*naranhha*
pineapple	piña†	*peenya*
lemonade	una limonada	*oona leemonada*
a glass of orangeade	un vaso de naranjada	*oon baso deh naranhhada*
milkshake	una malteada†	*oona malteada*
a smoothie	un batido/un licuado	*oon bateedo/oon leekwado*
sparkling/still mineral water	un agua mineral con gas/sin gas	*oon agwa meeneral kon gas/seen gas*

75

... milk	leche ...	*letcheh*
whole	entera	*entera*
semi-skimmed	semi descremada	*semee-deskremada*
skimmed	descremada	*deskremada*
soya	de soya†	*deh soya*

alcoholic drinks

a bottle of ... wine	una botella de vino ...	*oona boteya de beeno*
red	tinto	*teento*
white	blanco	*blanko*
a glass of rosé	una copa de vino rosado	*oona kopa deh beeno rosado*
brandy ...	brandy ...	*brandee*
with water	con agua	*kon agwa*
with soda	con soda	*kon soda*
cognac	un coñac	*oon konyak*
... beer	una cerveza ...	*oona serbesa*
dark	oscura	*oskoora*
light	clara	*klara*
foreign	importada	*eemportada*
local	nacional	*nasyonal*
gin (and tonic)	una ginebra (con tónica)	*oona hheenebra (kon toneeka)*
half a bottle of dry/ sweet wine	media botella de vino seco/dulce	*medya boteya deh beeno seko/doolseh*
pina colada	una piña colada	*oona peenya kolada*
(dry) martini	un martini (seco)	*oon marteenee (seko)*
port	un oporto	*oon oporto*
rum	un ron	*oon rron*
vermouth	un vermut	*oon bermoot*
vodka ...	un vodka ...	*oon bodka*
with a twist of lemon	con una rebanadita de limón	*kon oona rebanadeeta deh leemon*
whisky ...	un whisky ...	*oon weeskee*
neat	solo	*solo*
on the rocks	en las rocas	*en las rrokas*

Café **Life**

hot drinks

a cup of ...	una taza de ...	**oo**na **ta**sa deh
... coffee	un café ...	oon ka**feh**
black	negro	**ne**gro
white	con leche	kon **le**tcheh
decaffeinated	descafeinado	deska**fay**na**do**
espresso	exprés	es**pres**
weak	americano	amereeka**no**
camomile tea	té de manzanilla	teh deh mansa**nee**ya
cappuccino	un capuchino	oon kapoot**chee**no
hot chocolate	un chocolate	oon tchoko**la**teh
mint tea	té de yerbabuena†	teh deh yerba**bwe**na

tea with ...	un té negro con...	*oon teh **negro** kon*
lemon	limón	*lee**mon***
milk	leche	***le**tcheh*
Have you got any artificial sweetener?	¿Tiene sacarina/ endulzante?	*tyeneh saka**ree**na/ endool**san**teh*

ordering ice cream

What flavours do you have?	¿De qué sabores hay?	*deh keh sa**bo**res iy*
I'd like a ... ice cream.	Quisiera un helado de ...	*kee**sye**ra oon e**la**do deh*
chocolate	chocolate	*tchoko**la**te*
strawberry	fresa	***fre**sa*
vanilla	vainilla	*biy**nee**ya*
Could I have two ... sorbets?	¿Me puede dar dos granizados/sorbetes† de ...	*meh **pwe**deh dar dos granee**sa**dos/sor**be**tes deh*
mango	mango?	***man**go*
melon	melón?	***me**lon*
(see p59 for fruits)		
a ... cone	un barquillo† de ...	*oon bar**kee**yo deh*
coconut	coco	***ko**ko*
toffee	caramelo	*kara**me**lo*
a cup of ...	un vaso de ...	*oon **ba**so deh*
pistachio	pistacho	*pees**ta**tcho*
rum and raisin	ron con pasas	*rron kon **pa**sas*
a ... ice lolly	una paleta de ...	***oo**na pa**le**ta deh*
blackberry	mora	***mo**ra*
lemon	limón	*lee**mon***

check out 3

Ordering ice cream.

○ ¿Qué helados tienen?
keh elados tyenen

- De fresa, de limón y de piña.
deh fresa deh leemon ee deh peenya

○ ¿Tienen de chocolate?
tyenen deh tchokolateh

- Perdone, no tenemos.
perdoneh no tenemos

○ Quisiera un barquillo de fresa, por favor.
keesyera oon barkeeyo deh fresa por fabor

- Bueno.
bweno

 What ice cream flavour do they not have?

sound check

Spanish has some letters that don't exist in other languages:

ñ, pronounced like the 'ni' in 'onion':

| champaña | *tchampanya* | coñac | *konyak* |

ll, pronounced like the 'y' in 'yes':

| calle | *kayeh* | allí | *ayee* |

Practise these words:

| barquillo | *barkeeyo* | mañana | *manyana* |

try it out

crossword

Write the Spanish names of the five ice-cream flavours across the grid to help you work out the drink that America introduced to Europe.

	H							
	C							
	O							
	T							

1 toffee
2 blackberry
3 lemon
4 vanilla
5 melon

split the difference

Combine these word halves and find two that are not drinks.

1 te	**6** ca	**a** panada	**f** monada
2 re	**7** ja	**b** go	**g** quila
3 em	**8** le	**c** fé	**h** fresco
4 ju	**9** cer	**d** món	**i** che
5 li		**e** veza	

as if you were there

Follow the prompts to order food and drinks in a café.

Buenas tardes, ¿Qué van a tomar?

(Ask for a tea with milk and ask what soft drinks they have)
Tenemos jugo de naranja, limonada y agua mineral.

(Ask for a lemonade)
¿Es todo?

(Ask for two corn pastries)
Perdone, no tenemos.

(Ask for some crisps)

... **link**up

¿Quisiera un café, por favor.	**I'd like** a coffee, please.
Me puede dar una porción de papas fritas?	**Can I have** a portion of crisps/chips?
¿Tiene aceitunas?	**Do you have** any olives?
¿Qué refrescos **tiene?**	**What** cold drinks **do you have?**
Para mí una limonada.	A lemonade **for me.**

requesting things

The easiest way is simply to say what you want:
Dos cervezas, por favor.   Two beers, please.

You can also say:
Para mí, una cerveza.   A beer for me.

Otherwise you can use ¿Me puede dar ...? (literally, 'Can you give me ...?') or ¿Me puede traer ...? (literally, 'Can you bring me ...?'):

¿Me puede dar una cerveza, por favor?
Please could I have a beer?

¿Me puede traer una cerveza, por favor?
Please would you bring me a beer?

Eating **Out**

when to eat

The most important meal of the day is lunch (**almuerzo**), eaten between 2 and 4pm. The best bet is to join the locals and get the fixed-price menu (**menú del día**).

Breakfast (**desayuno**) varies considerably, from the skimpy breakfasts offered in cheap hotels to the staple of beans, rice, eggs, meat and maize pancakes (**arepas**) common in Central America and some Andean countries.

Dinner (**cena** – **merienda** in Ecuador) is served after 6pm, although in the Southern Cone's hotter months (January and February) hardly any restaurant opens for dinner before 8pm. The choice of local and international cuisine is generally plentiful.

where to eat

Marisquería A type of fish restaurant found on the Chilean coast. Chilean fish and seafood rank among the best in the world.

Paladar A Cuban home restaurant. Eating out in Cuba can be difficult due to food shortages, so **paladares** are a good way to taste the local food and avoid the tourist traps.

Rosticería/pollería/asadero de pollos are roast-chicken outlets. They will usually have a child-friendly menu.

Café is the general term for cheaper places to eat. Some regional variations of inexpensive eateries are:

Cocina económica in Mexico; if you want to mingle with the locals, this is the place to go.

Comedor A Central American restaurant. In remote areas, it may only be a simple shack where food is cooked over a wood fire.

Pupusería A restaurant or café in El Salvador where **pupusas** (thick, corn tortillas filled with anything from meat to refried beans) are sold.

Fritanga is both a type of food, very common in Nicaragua and other Central American countries, and the place where it is sold. You will find deep-fried meat or

fish, sliced plantains, cheese, and so on.

Soda is a Costa Rican term for 'greasy spoon'. Most have ready-to-eat food, and you can't beat the prices.

what to eat

Most traditional dishes (**platos típicos**) are a **mestizo** creation, a combination of indigenous cooking and Spanish influence.

Ceviche Mostly found in Peru, Ecuador, and Colombia and consisting of raw fish, prawns, scallops or squid, or a mixture of all of these, marinated in lime juice and chilli peppers.

Mole poblano Prepared with dried chilli peppers, ground nuts, spices and chocolate sauce, **mole poblano** is regarded as Mexico's national dish.

Asado or parrillada A mix of barbecued or chargrilled cuts of succulent Argentinian beef. It usually comes with heaps of salad and chips.

Cuy The famous roasted or grilled guinea pig is a speciality of Ecuadorian highlands and southern Colombia.

Tacos, burritos, enchiladas Baked or fried, these Mexican specialities are found throughout the region. Consisting of soft maize or wheat tortillas, or hard taco shells, they come stuffed with a variety of fillings.

dietary requirements

Vegetarian restaurants are few and far between, so your best bet is to choose the vegetable options available on most menus.

Be aware that some seemingly vegetarian meals may turn out to include unwanted ingredients. Some Latin Americans may have a different understanding of the words vegetarian and vegan, so also make it clear that you do not eat poultry and fish.

For vegetarian restaurants in the region, visit **www.vrg.org/travel/larg.htm#Restaurants**.

phrasemaker

finding a place to eat

you may say …

Is there a good restaurant near here?	¿Hay un buen restaurante por aquí?	*iy oon bwen restowranteh por akee*
Can you recommend a traditional restaurant?	¿Me puede recomendar un restaurante típico?	*meh pwedeh rekomendar oon restowranteh teepeeko*
I'd like to book a table for …	Quisiera reservar una mesa para …	*keesyera reserbar oona mesa para*
two.	dos personas.	*dos personas*
tonight	esta noche.	*esta notcheh*
Tuesday.	el martes.	*el martes*
at …	a …	*a*
eight	las ocho	*las otcho*
half past eight (see p13 for time)	las ocho y media	*las otcho ee medya*
in the name of …	a nombre de …	*a nombreh deh*

you may hear …

No hace falta reservar.	*no aseh falta reserbar*	There's no need to book.
¿Para cúantas personas?	*para kwantas personas*	For how many people?
Está bien.	*esta byen*	That's fine.
Perdón, está lleno.	*perdon esta yeno*	Sorry, we're full.

arriving

you may say …

We have a reservation.	Tenemos una reservación/una reserva†.	*tenemos oona reserbasyon/oona reserba*
a table …	una mesa …	*oona mesa*
by the window	junto a la ventana	*hhoonto a la bentana*
outside/inside	afuera/adentro	*afwera/adentro*
in the (no) smoking area	en la sección de (no) fumar	*en la seksyon deh (no) foomar*

Eating **Out**

Do you have a high chair?	¿Tiene una silla para niños?	*tyeneh oona seeya para neenyos*

you may hear ...

Bienvenido(s).	*byen-beneedo(s)*	Welcome.
Pase(n) por aquí.	*pase(n) por akee*	Please come this way.
Espere(n), por favor.	*espere(n) por fabor*	You'll have to wait.

check out 1
You phone to book a table at a restaurant.

- Hacienda de Los Morales, buenas tardes.
  asyenda deh los morales bwenas tardes

○ Buenas tardes, quisiera reservar una mesa para mañana por la noche.
  bwenas tardes keesyera reserbar oona mesa para manyana por la notcheh

- Mañana por la noche ... perdone pero no tenemos por la noche.
  manyana por la notcheh ... perdoneh pero no tenemos por la notcheh

○ ¿Para el jueves?
  para el hhwebes

- Para el jueves ... está bien, señora. ¿Para cuántas personas?
  para el hhwebes ... esta byen senyora. para kwantas personas

○ Para tres, a las ocho.
  para tres a las otcho

- Bueno. Hasta el jueves, señora.
  bweno. asta el hhwebes senyora

Q There aren't any tables available tomorrow night: true/false?
You book a table for eight at three o'clock: true/false?

asking about the menu

you may say ...

The menu, please.	La carta, por favor.	*la **kar**ta por fa**bor***
Is there ...	¿Hay ...	*iy*
a set menu?	menú del día?	*me**noo** del **dee**a*
a children's menu?	menú infantil?	*me**noo** eenfan**teel***
What's the ...	¿Cuál es ...	*kwal es*
soup of the day?	la sopa del día?	*la **so**pa del **dee**a*
local speciality?	el plato típico de	*el **pla**to **tee**peeko*
	aquí?	*deh a**kee***
What do you recommend?	¿Qué me recomienda?	*keh meh reco**myen**da*
What is/are ...?	¿Qué es/son ...?	*keh es/son*
What is/are ... like?	¿Cómo es/son ...?	***ko**mo es/son*
What does it/do they contain?	¿Qué lleva/llevan?	*keh **yeb**a/**yeb**an*
Is it (very) spicy?	¿Pica (mucho)?	***pee**ka (**moo**tcho)*
Do you have any ...	¿Tienen ...	***tye**nen*
seafood?	comida de mar?	*ko**mee**da deh mar*
vegetarian dishes?	platos vegetarianos?	***pla**tos behheta**rya**nos*
I'm allergic to ...	Soy alérgico/a ...	*soy a**lerhheeko**/a*
nuts.	a las nueces.	*a las **nwe**ses*
shellfish.	a los mariscos.	*a los ma**rees**kos*
I don't eat ...	No como ...	*no **ko**mo*
meat.	carne.	***kar**neh*
dairy products.	lácteos.	***lak**teos*
I'm ...	Soy ...	*soy*
vegetarian.	vegetariano/a.	*behheta**rya**no/a*
vegan.	végano/a.	***beg**ano/a*
Does it contain ...	Lleva	***yeb**a*
chilli?	ají/chile?	*a**hhee**/**tchee**leh*
wheat?	trigo?	***tree**go*
Has the salad been disinfected?	¿La ensalada está desinfectada?	*la ensa**la**da es**ta** deseenfek**ta**da*
Is it purified water?	¿Es agua purificada?	*es **a**gwa pooreefee**ka**da*

Eating **Out**

you may hear ...

Tenemos ...
  un menú turístico.
 	
  un almuerzo bufé.
	tenemos
	  oon menoo
	  tooreesteeko
	  oon almwerso
	  boofeh
		We have ...
		  a tourist menu.
		
		  a lunch buffet.

Es a la carta.	es a la karta	It's a la carte.

Es una especie de ...
  pescado blanco.
  estofado.
	es oona espesyeh deh
	  peskado blanko
	  estofado
		It's a sort of ...
		  white fish.
		  stew.

Son un tipo de ...
  semilla.
  verdura.
	son oon teepo deh
	  semeeya
	  berdoora
		They're a type of ...
		  seed.
		  vegetable.

Lleva ...
  pollo.
  una salsa cremosa.
	yeba
	  poyo
	  oona salsa kremosa
		It's made with ...
		  chicken.
		  a creamy sauce.

Se lo recomiendo.	seh lo rekomyendo	I recommend it.
Sí, pica (un poco).	see peeka (oon poko)	Yes, it's (a bit) spicy.
No, no pica.	no no peeka	No, it's not spicy.

check out 2

You're in a Mexican restaurant asking about one of the local specialities.

○ ¿Y de plato principal?
ee deh plato preenseepal

- ¿Cómo es el huachinango a la veracruzana?
komo es el watcheenango a la berakroosana

○ Es un pescado al horno guisado con tomate, cebolla, chiles y aceitunas. Se lo recomiendo.
es oon peskado al orno geesado kon tomateh seboya tcheeles ee asaytoonas. seh lo rekomyendo

 What is in huachinango a la veracruzana?

ordering

you may say ...

Waiter/Waitress!	¡Mesero!/¡Mesera†!	*mesero/mesera*
Excuse me!	¡Disculpe!/¡Perdone!	*deeskoolpeh/perdoneh*

... for me.
  A fish soup
	Para mí ...
	  una sopa de pescado.
		para mee
		  oona sopa deh peskado

Chicken tacos	unos tacos de pollo.	*oonos takos deh poyo*
To start with, I'm going to have ...	Para empezar, voy a tomar ...	*para empesar boy a tomar*
As a main course, I'd like ...	Como plato principal, quisiera ...	*komo plato preenseepal keesyera*
For dessert, I'll have ...	De postre, me puede dar ...	*deh postreh meh pwedeh dar*
Could we have a bottle of red wine? (see drinks, p75)	¿Nos puede dar una botella de vino tinto?	*nos pwedeh dar oona boteya deh beeno teento*
rare†	poco hecho/a	*poko etcho/a*
medium†	término medio	*termeeno medyo*
well done†	bien hecho/a	*byen etcho/a*

you may hear ...

¿Le(s) tomo su orden?	*les tomo soo orden*	Shall I take your order?
¿Qué van a tomar?	*keh ban a tomar*	What would you like?
Perdone, no tenemos ...	*perdoneh no tenemos*	Sorry, we haven't got any ...
¿Cómo lo quiere?	*komo lo kyereh*	How would you like it?

Eating **Out**

¿Van a tomar postre/ café?	*ban a tomar postreh/ kafeh*	Would you like any dessert/coffee?
¿Quieren algo de beber?	*kyeren algo deh beber*	Would you like anything to drink?
¿Y de beber?	*ee deh beber*	Anything to drink?
Sí, claro./Sí, cómo no.	*see klaro/see komo no*	Yes, of course.

check out 3

You and a friend are deciding what to order.

– ¿Les tomo su orden?
  les tomo soo orden

○ Sí. ¿Qué lleva el ceviche?
  see keh yeba el sebeetcheh

– Pescado o mariscos, limón, cebolla y tomates.
  peskado o mareeskos leemon seboya ee tomates

○ No, gracias. Soy alérgico a los mariscos. ¿La ensalada está desinfectada?
  no grasyas soy alerhheeko a los mareeskos. la ensalada esta deseenfektada

– Sí, claro.
  see klaro

○ Una ensalada césar y ... enchiladas suizas. ¿Pican mucho?
  oona ensalada sesar ee ... entcheeladas sweesas. peekan mootcho

– No, no pican.
  no no peekan

○ Bueno, unas enchiladas suizas.
  bweno oonas entcheeladas sweesas

Q Why can't you eat the ceviche?
Are the enchiladas hot?

during the meal

you may say ...

Could you bring me ... please?	¿Me puede traer ... por favor?	meh **pwe**deh tra**er** ... por fa**bor**
a knife	un cuchillo	oon koo**tchee**yo
more bread	más pan	mas pan
This is not what I asked for.	Esto no es lo que pedí.	**es**to no es lo keh pe**dee**
I asked for ...	Pedí ...	pe**dee**
It's ...	Está ...	es**ta**
cold.	frío	**free**o
raw.	crudo.	**kroo**do
delicious.	rico.	**rree**ko
It's/They're very spicy!	¡Pica/Pican mucho!	**pee**ka/**pee**kan **moo**tcho
Can you change this ...	¿Me puede cambiar este ...	meh **pwe**deh kam**byar es**teh
fork?	tenedor?	tene**dor**
dish?	plato?	**pla**to
Where are the toilets?	¿Dónde están los baños?	**don**deh es**tan** los **ba**nyos

you may hear ...

¿Todo está bien?	**to**do es**ta** byen	Is everything all right?
Ya le traigo ...	ya leh **triy**go	I'll bring you ...
más agua.	mas **a**gwa	more water.
hielo.	**ye**lo	some ice.
Disculpe, ya le traigo otro/otra	dees**kool**peh ya leh **triy**go **o**tro/**o**tra	Sorry, I'll bring you another one.
¡Enseguida!	ense**gee**da	Straight away!

Eating **Out**

on your table

ashtray	el cenicero	*el seneesero*
bowl	el tazón	*el tason*
cup	la taza†	*la tasa*
fork	el tenedor	*el tenedor*
glass	el vaso	*el baso*
jug	la jarra	*la hharra*
knife	el cuchillo	*el kootcheeyo*
napkin	la servilleta	*la serbeeyeta*
pepper	la pimienta	*la peemyenta*
plate	el plato	*el plato*
salt shaker	el salero	*el salero*
saucer	el platico	*el plateeko*
spoon	la cuchara	*la kootchara*
teaspoon	la cucharita	*la kootchareeta*
wine glass	la copa	*la kopa*

paying the bill

you may say ...

The bill, please.	La cuenta, por favor.	*la kwenta por fabor*
Is service included?	¿Está incluido el servicio?	*esta eenklweedo el serbeesyo*
Do you take credit cards?	¿Aceptan tarjetas de crédito?	*aseptan tarhhetas deh kredeeto*
There's a mistake.	Hay un error.	*iy oon error*
We didn't have this.	No pedimos esto.	*no pedeemos esto*
Keep the change.	Quédese con el cambio.	*kehdeseh kon el kambyo*

you may hear ...

El servicio está incluido/es aparte	*el serbeesyo esta eenklweedo/es aparteh*	Service is included/extra.

sound check

g + **e** or **i** is pronounced like the 'ch' in 'loch':

Argentina   *arhhen**tee**na*   ginebra   *hhee**ne**bra*

g + **ue** or **ui** is pronounced like the 'g' in 'gun'. In these cases, the **u** is silent:

guitarra   *gee**ta**rra*   portugués   *portoo**ges***

g + any other combination of letters is pronounced like the 'g' in 'gun', with all the following letters pronounced.

agua   ***a**gwa*   gracias   ***gra**syas*

Practise with these words:

guacamole *gwaka**mo**leh* gelatina *hhela**tee**na* guerra ***ge**rra*

try it out

get it right!

What do you say when you ...
  a   have a reservation in your name
  b   need a high chair
  c   want to know if the food is spicy/hot
  d   are allergic to dairy
  e   get the wrong order
  f   want more bread

Eating **Out**

on the menu

Choose one set menu for both you and your friend. You don't like fish and your friend is allergic to nuts.

Menu 1

sopa de verduras
pescado frito
helado de vainilla

Menu 2

ceviche
pollo con papas
torta de manzana y nueces

Menu 3

ensalada verde
estofado de carne
flan de chocolate

as if you were there

You've been out for a walk by the sea and want to stop for dinner. Order your meal according to the prompts.

(Greet the waiter and say you'd like a table for two)
Muy bien. Por aquí. ¿Qué van a tomar?
(Ask for a bottle of red wine and some chicken tacos)
¿Quieren agua?
(Ask if the water is purified)
Sí, cómo no.

linkup

key phrases

¿Qué es el ceviche?	**What is** *ceviche*?
¿Cómo son las enchiladas suizas?	**What are** the *enchiladas suizas* **like?**
Voy a tomar el pollo.	**I'm going to have** the chicken.
Para mí la ensalada.	The salad **for me.**
¿Me puede traer más café, por favor?	**Could you bring me** more coffee, please?

talking to you

In Latin American Spanish when talking to one person, there are three words for 'you', usted, tú and vos. The formal/polite word is usted; the more friendly words are tú or vos. (Vos is a regional variation, particularly common in Argentina and Uruguay).

The word itself may often be missed out, but the one you choose determines the ending you put on the verb.

A waiter would say to you:

¿Qué quiere tomar? What would you like? (formal)

But to a friend or someone you know fairly well, you'd say:

¿Qué quieres tomar? What would you like? (informal tu form)
¿Qué querés tomar? What would you like? (informal vos form)

Eating **Out**

With the usted form, the ending of the verb is usually an **-a** or an **-e**:

¿Dónde vive? Where do you live?
¿Dónde trabaja? Where do you work?

If you choose the tú form, there's an **-s** at the end:

¿Dónde vives? Where do you live?
¿Dónde trabajas? Where do you work?

If you choose the vos form, there's an **-s** at the end and an accent on the final vowel.

¿Dónde vivís?   Where do you live?
¿Dónde trabajás? Where do you work?

Things change if you are talking to more than one person:

¿Dónde viven (ustedes)? Where do you (e.g. both) live?
¿Dónde trabajan (ustedes)? Where do you (e.g. two) work?

For more on 'you', see the Language Builder, p133. ·····⟩

saying what you are going to do

To say what you're **going to** do, use Voy a ('I'm going to') or Vamos a ('We're going to') followed by an infinitive (the part of the verb you'll find in a dictionary, ending in **-ar, -er** or **-ir**):

Voy a pedir el pescado.   I'm going to have the fish.
Vamos a tomar una copa. We're going to have a drink.

And if someone asks you what you're going to do, you'll hear Va a (or Van a if you're in a group):

¿Va a tomar postre? Are you going to have dessert?

menus & courses

plato del día	set menu of the day
entradas/entrantes	appetizers, starters
platos principales	main courses
carnes	meat
caza y aves	game and poultry
pescados (y mariscos)	fish (and shellfish)
platos vegetarianos	vegetarian dishes
ensaladas	salads
verduras y legumbres	vegetables and pulses
agregados/porciones/refacciones	side orders
bebidas	drinks
licores	alcoholic drinks
tabla de quesos	cheese board
postres	desserts

main styles of cooking

a la moda	with ice cream
a la parrilla/a la plancha	grilled
a la romana	deep fried in batter
al carbón	chargrilled
al gusto	to your taste
al horno	in the oven: baked/roasted
al mojo de ajo	grilled with garlic
al vapor	steamed
apanado/a	breaded
asado/a	roast

empanizado/a	breaded
en salsa	in a sauce
encebollado/a	with onions
encurtido/a	pickled
frito/a	deep fried
gratinado/a	with melted cheese
guisado/a	stewed
hervido/a	boiled
relleno/a	stuffed

the menu

almejas	clams
anticucho	chargrilled skewers of beef heart, served with a hot sauce
arenque (ahumado)	(smoked) herring
arepa	flat cornmeal patty, eaten plain or stuffed
arroz	rice
blanco	white
atollado	with meat and spices
congrí	with black beans
atún	tuna
avena	porridge/milky oatmeal drink
bacalao	cod (usually dried)
barbacoa	leg of lamb wrapped in cactus leaves and cooked slowly
bife	steak
bistec (a caballo)	steak (topped with fried eggs)
boquerones	whitebait
brocheta	brochette
cabrito	kid
calamares	squid
en su tinta	in their ink
caldo tlalpeño	chicken consommé with avocado
caldo/consomé de pollo	chicken consommé
camarones	prawns/shrimps
cangrejo	crab
carne a la tampiqueña	steak served with guacamole, a quesadilla and fried beans
carne de res	beef

carnero	lamb
carnitas	pork cooked in a copper pot
cerdo	pork
ceviche	marinated fish/seafood
conejo	rabbit
cordero	lamb
costilla	rib
crema de tomate	tomato soup
chancho	pork
chinchulines	chitterlings
chipi chipi	soup made with tiny clams
chivo	lamb
chompipe	turkey
chorizo	very spicy pork sausage
chuleta	chop
chupe	chowder
churrasco	large grilled steak
enchiladas	stuffed wheat-flour pancakes
ensalada	salad
rusa	Russian (diced potatoes and vegetables with mayonnaise)
espaguetis a la mantequilla	spaghetti in butter sauce
faisán	pheasant
fajitas de filete miñón	strips of filet mignon sautéed with onions and peppers, served with wheat tortillas
filete de pescado	fillet steak
gazpacho	cold, spicy soup made with tomatoes
guacamole	purée of avocados, tomatoes, onions and coriander
guajolote	turkey
hayacas	parcels of maize dough filled with meat and vegetables
hígado	liver
huachinango	red snapper
huevos	eggs
revueltos/duros	scrambled/hard-boiled
rancheros	fried served on tortillas with tomato and chilli sauce
jaibas	crab
langosta	lobster

langostinos	crayfish/king prawns
lenguado	sole
lomo	loin
machaca	shredded beef or pork
marrano	pork
merluza	hake
mero	bass
mojarra	type of sea bream/tilapia fish
mole	meat in a sauce made with herbs, nuts, spices and chilli
molletes con frijoles	toasted bread rolls topped with fried beans and melted cheese
moros y cristianos	dark beans with white rice
pabellón criollo	rice, bean and meat stew
pan	bread
panceta	bacon
pargo	red snapper
pato	duck
pavo	turkey
pez espada	swordfish
pierna	leg
pollo	chicken
higaditos/corazones	livers/hearts
pechuga/pernil	breast/thighs
pierna	drumstick
puerco	pork
pulpo	octopus
quesadillas	folded filled tortillas
queso fundido	grilled cheese
riñones	kidneys
róbalo	sea bass
salchichas	sausages
salmón	salmon
salmonete	red mullet
sardinas	sardines
sopa	soup
de fideos	pasta or noodle
de lentejas	lentil
tacos	rolled filled tortillas
tamales	parcels of maize dough filled with meat and a sauce
ternera	veal

tocino	bacon
tortillas	corn pancakes
tostadas	toast
tostadas (Mexico)	tortillas topped with beans, lettuce, meat, cheese, cream and salsa
trucha	trout
venado	venison
vinagre	vinegar
viudo de pescado	fish stew

desserts

alfajores	biscuits with caramel sauce or jam, covered with icing sugar
arequipe/dulce de leche/ manjar blanco	milk-based syrup (either a sauce or a caramel-like sweet)
arroz de leche	rice pudding
ate	fruit jelly
bisquets con mantequilla y miel	scones with butter and honey
brazo gitano	sponge cake with cream filling
crepas de cajeta	pancakes with sweet caramelised milk
chongos zamoranos	milk, cinnamon and sugar
flan de coco	coconut crème caramel
fruta de la estación	seasonal fruit
gelatina	jelly
pastel	cake
pay/pie	pie
plato de fruta con yogurt	platter of fruit with yoghurt
pudín de zanahoria	carrot cake/pudding
queque/torta	cake
tarta (Argentina)	pie
tarta de almendras y nueces	almond and walnut cake

Entertainment

finding out what's on

Latin American embassies can be a good source of information, and each country has an official tourism website in English.

Once you're there, visit the local tourist office for information or check the newspaper kiosks for entertainment guides (**guía de entretenimientos, guía de espectaculos** or **guía del ocio**), although these will almost certainly only be published in Spanish.

ruins

The awe-inspiring ruins of some of the largest pre-Columbian civilisations can be found in Mexico, Guatemala and Peru: the Mayan and Aztec remains of Teotihuacán, Chichén Itzá and Palenque in Mexico and Tikal in eastern Guatemala, and the ceremonial Inca city of Machu Picchu in Peru.

national parks

From the Iguazú Falls to Tierra del Fuego, the breathtaking sights of Argentina's many national parks have found their way onto UNESCO's World Heritage List. Many parks have camping areas.

the Amazon

Rich in wildlife and vegetation, **the Amazon is a** nature-lover's **paradise**. Take a long boat trip down the Amazon River or, if you're pressed for time, enjoy a day's exploring by canoe. **Visiting the national parks in the region is the best and safest way to get the most out of your trip.**

festivals

One of the most vibrant of Latin American festivals is **Semana Santa** (Holy Week), which ends on Easter Sunday and is best seen in Guatemala. The Peruvian Inca tradition, Inti Raymi, is a must-see, as are the Independence Day festivities in Mexico, the Feast of

San Jeronim in Nicaragua and the colourful children's parade, **Paso del Niño Viajero**, in Ecuador. Day of the Dead celebrations are at their most spectacular in Mexico and Guatemala.

music

The Caribbean exists on a diet of music, and countries such as Venezuela, Colombia and Ecuador have **salsa** and **merengue** rhythms in their blood. Argentina's most famous musical tradition is the **tango**. Head to an **espectáculo** (show) for a highly choreographed display or, for a more local flavour, visit one of the dance halls for regular events (**milongas**).

Throughout Latin America you will also find **Mariachi** street entertainers, in their typical silver-studded **charro** costumes and wide-brimmed hats.

sport

Football is the biggest spectator sport in the region. The season runs from July to December but there are matches all year round.

Skiing Argentina and Chile are the places to go for skiing. The season runs from late May to early October. For updates and conditions, check **www.andesweb.com**.

Diving The Caribbean coasts and islands are surrounded by living reefs, providing excellent diving. Many tour operators have special packages for boat dives, equipment rental and diving instruction.

Bullfighting (corrida de toros) is one of the best-known and certainly the most controversial of Hispanic traditions. The most pro-bullfighting Latin American country is Mexico, followed by Colombia and Venezuela. However, the sport is forbidden in Argentina, Chile, Uruguay and Cuba.

children

Visitors to Latin America can find well-organised water parks in resort areas, zoos, fun fairs, and interactive museums for older children.

phrasemaker

getting to know the place

you may say ...

Do you have ...	¿Tiene ...	*tyeneh*
a plan of the town	un mapa/plano de la ciudad?	*oon mapa/plano deh la syoodath*
an entertainment guide?	una guía de espectáculos?	*oona geea deh espektakoolos*
information in English?	información en inglés?	*eenformasyon en eengles*
What is there to see/do here?	¿Qué hay para ver/hacer aquí?	*keh iy para berlaser akee*
Is there a ...	¿Hay ...	*iy*
swimming pool?	una piscina†?	*oona peeseena*
guided tour?	una visita con guía?	*oona beeseeta kon geea*
museum?	un museo?	*oon mooseo*
Are there any ...	¿Hay ...	*iy*
parks?	algún parque?	*algoon parkeh*
beaches?	alguna playa?	*algoona playa*
Is there anything for children?	¿Hay algo para niños?	*iy algo para neenyos*
Can you recommend ...	¿Puede recomendarme ...	*pwedeh rekomendarmeh*
a nightclub?	una discoteca†?	*oona deeskoteka*
a show?	un espectáculo?	*oon espektakoolo*
an art gallery?	una galería de arte?	*oona galereea deh arteh*
Where is the ...	¿Dónde está ...	*dondeh esta*
tourist office?	la oficina de turismo?	*la ofeeseena deh tureesmo*
cathedral?	la catedral?	*la katedral*
the sea?	el mar?	*el mar*
Where are ...	¿Dónde están ...	*dondeh estan*
the pyramids?	las pirámides?	*las peerameedes*
the lakes?	los lagos?	*los lagos*

you may hear ...

Hay un tour en autobus† ...	*iy oon toor en owto**boos***	There's a bus tour ...
todos los días.	*to**dos** los **dee**as*	every day.
los fines de semana.	*los **fee**nes deh sema**na***	at weekends.
Hay ruinas/iglesias muy interesantes.	*iy rwee**nas**/eegle**syas** mwee eentere**san**tes*	There are some very interesting ruins/ churches.
Puede visitar ...	*pwedeh beesee**tar***	You can visit ...
una cascada.	*oona kas**ka**da*	a waterfall.
un templo.	*oon **templo***	a temple.
... está aquí.	*esta a**kee***	... is here.
El centro turístico	*el **sen**tro too**rees**teeko*	The resort
El balneario	*el bal**nea**ryo*	The spa
Le recomiendo ...	*leh rreko**myen**do*	I'd recommend ...
la excursión en bicicleta.	*la eskoor**syon** en beesee**kle**ta*	the bike excursion.
las aguas termales.	*las a**gwas** ter**ma**les*	the thermal baths.
Hay una exposición de ...	*iy **oo**na esposee**syon** deh*	There is ... exhibition.
arte.	*ar**teh***	an art
pintura.	*peen**too**ra*	a painting

talking about your interests
you may say ...

I'd like to go to the cinema/theatre.	Me gustaría ir al cine/al teatro.	*meh goosta**ree**a eer al **see**neh/al te**a**tro*
I like/don't like ...	Me gusta/no me gusta ...	*meh **goos**ta/no meh **goos**ta*
dancing.	bailar.	*biy**lar***
archaeology.	la arqueología.	*la arkeolo**hhee**a*
I like/don't like ...	Me gustan/no me gustan ...	*meh **goos**tan/no meh **goos**tan*
parades.	los desfiles.	*los des**fee**les*
local festivals.	las fiestas.	*las **fyes**tas*

I'm interested in ...	Me interesa ...	*meh eenteresa*
football.	el fútbol.	*el footbol*
ecotourism.	el ecoturismo.	*el eko-tooreesmo*

you may hear ...

¿Qué le gusta?	*keh leh goosta*	What do you like?
¿Le gusta la salsa/el montañismo?	*leh goosta la salsa/el montanyeesmo*	Do you like salsa/ mountaineering?
¿Le gustan los fuegos artificiales/las ferias de diversiones?	*leh goostan los fwegos arteefeesyales/las ferya deh deebersyones*	Do you like fireworks/funfairs?

check out 1

In the Tourist Office you find out there are mummies in Mexico.

○ ¿Qué hay para ver aquí en Guanajuato?
keh iy para ber akee en gwanahhwato

– Puede visitar el Museo Casa Diego Rivera y el Museo de las Momias.
pwedeh beeseetar el mooseo kasa dyego rreebera ee el mooseo deh las momyas

○ ¿Momias?
momyas

– Sí. Hay una visita con guía todos los días.
see. iy oona beeseeta kon geea todos los deeas

○ Gracias.
grasyas   (momias = mummies)

Q How often is the guided tour of the mummy museum?

getting more information

you may say ...

What are the opening times?	¿Cuál es el horario?	kwal es el oraryo
Are the films dubbed or do they have subtitles?	¿Las películas son dobladas o tienen subtítulos?	las peleekoolas son dobladas o tyenen soobteetoolos
Where does the tour go?	¿Adónde va el tour?	adondeh ba el toor
What time does the football match start/finish?	¿A qué hora empieza/termina el partido de fútbol?	a keh ora empyesa/ termeena el parteedo deh footbol
Is there wheelchair access?	¿Hay acceso para personas en silla de ruedas?	iy akseso para personas en seeya deh rwedas
How long does it last?	¿Cuánto dura?	kwanto doora
Is there an interval?	¿Hay intermedio?	iy eentermedyo
Do you need tickets?	¿Se necesitan entradas/boletos*?	seh neseseetan entradas
Where do you buy tickets for the ... concert? race?	¿Dónde se compran las entradas para ... el concierto? la carrera?	dondeh seh kompran las entradas para el konsyerto la karrera

you may hear ...

Abre ... de diez de la mañana a seis de la tarde.	abreh deh dyes deh la manyana a says deh la tardeh	It's open ... from 10am till 6pm.
todos los días excepto el domingo.	todos los deeas esepto el domeengo	every day except Sunday.
Está cerrado ... los lunes. en invierno.	esta serrado los loones en eenbyerno	It's closed ... on Mondays. in winter.
Va a ...	ba a	It goes to ...
Para en ...	para en	It stops at ...

Empieza/termina a la(s) ...	empyesa/termeena a la(s)	It starts/finishes at ...
Dura tres horas.	doora tres oras	It lasts three hours.
No se necesitan entradas.	no seh neseseetan entradas	You don't need tickets.
Es gratis.	es gratees	It's free.
Puede comprarlas ... en la taquilla/ ventanilla. en la puerta. aquí.	pwedeh komprarlas en la takeeya/ bentaneeya, en la pwerta akee	You can buy them ... at the ticket office. on the door. here.

(*When talking about transport, the word for 'ticket' is billete beeyeteh or pasaje pasahheh.)

check out 2

You ask about tours to Machu Picchu in your Cuzco hotel.

○ ¿Hay tours a Machu Picchu?
  iy toors a matchoo peetchoo

– Hay uno todos los días.
  iy oono todos los deeas

○ ¿A qué hora empieza?
  a keh ora empyesa

– A las siete de la mañana.
  a las syeteh deh la manyana

○ ¿Y dónde se compran los boletos?
  ee dondeh seh kompran los boletos

– Aquí.
  akee

Q What time does the tour start?
Where can you buy a ticket?

getting in

you may say ...

Are there any tickets for the concert?	¿Hay entradas para el concierto?	*iy entradas para el konsyerto*
Are there any tickets for tonight/ tomorrow?	¿Hay entradas para esta noche/mañana?	*iy entradas para esta notcheh/manyana*
What does the multiple pass include?	¿Qué incluye la entrada múltiple?	*keh eenklooyeh la entrada moolteepleh*
How much is it for a group ticket?	¿Cuánto cuestan las entradas para grupos?	*kwanto kwestan las entradas para groopos*
Is there a concession for ... senior citizens? people with disabilities? students?	¿Hay descuentos para adultos mayores? discapacitados? estudiantes?	*iy deskwentos para adooltos mayores* *deeskapaseetados* *estoodyantes*
One adult and two children, please.	Un adulto y dos niños, por favor.	*oon adoolto ee dos neenyos por fabor*
Two stalls/gallery tickets, please.	Dos entradas de platea/galería por favor	*dos entradas deh platea/galereea por fabor*
I'd like to buy a programme.	Quisiera comprar un programa.	*keesyera komprar oon programa*
Where is the cloakroom?	¿Dónde está el guardarropa?	*dondeh esta el gwarda-rropa*

Entertainment

you may hear ...

Perdone, están agotados/as.	*perdoneh estan agotados/as*	Sorry, it's sold out.
Los extranjeros/los visitantes locales pagan ...	*los estranhheros/los beeseetantes lokales pagan*	The price for foreign/local visitors is ...

sports
you may say ...

Where can you play ...	¿Dónde se puede jugar ...	*dondeh seh pwedeh hhoogar*
tennis?	al tenis?	*al tenees*
golf?	al golf?	*al golf*
Where can you go ...	¿Dónde se puede ...	*dondeh seh pwedeh*
hiking?	hacer caminatas?	*aser kameenatas*
fishing?	pescar?	*peskar*
snorkelling?	bucear con esnórkel?	*boosear kon esnorkel*
skiing?	esquiar?	*eskyar*
horseriding?	montar a caballo?	*montar a kabayo*
Can I hire ...	¿Se puede alquilar ...	*seh pwedeh alkeelar*
a racket?	una raqueta?	*oona rraketa*
a sun lounger?	una silla de playa/una reposera?	*oona seeya deh playa/oona reposera*
some flippers and a mask?	unas aletas y un visor?	*oonas aletas ee oon beesor*
a windsurf board?	una tabla de windsurf?	*oona tabla deh weensorf*
a mountain bike?	una bicicleta de montaña?	*oona beeseekleta deh montanya*
I'd like to take ... lessons.	Me gustaría tomar clases de ...	*meh goostareea tomar klases deh*
diving	buceo.	*booseo*
sailing	navegación a vela.	*nabegasyon a bela*
Is it safe to swim here?	¿Es seguro nadar aquí?	*es segooro nadar akee*

Is it ...	¿Es ...	es
okay for beginners?	apto para principiantes?	apto para preenseepyantes
difficult/dangerous?	difícil/peligroso?	deefeeseel/ peleegroso

Where are the ...	¿Dónde están ...	dondeh estan
changing rooms?	los vestidores?	los besteedores
lockers?	los casilleros?	los kaseeyeros

you may hear ...

Cuesta treinta pesos el día/la hora	kwesta traynta pesos el deea/la ora	It's 30 pesos a day/ an hour.
¿Necesita un guía/ unas pelotas?	neseseeta oon geea/ oonas pelotas	Do you want a guide/ some balls?
Hay ... cerca de la playa.	iy ... serka deh la playa	There is ... near the beach.
golfito	golfeeto	mini-golf
una cancha de tenis	oona kantcha deh tenees	a tennis court

check out 3

You decide to try your hand at snorkelling.

○ ¿Se puede alquilar un visor?
  seh pwedeh alkeelar oon beesor

– Sí, claro. ¿Quiere el visor solo o con aletas?
  see klaro. kyereh el beesor solo o kon aletas

○ ¿Cuánto cuesta con aletas?
  kwanto kwesta kon aletas

– Cuarenta pesos la hora.
  kwarenta pesos la ora

○ Bien, me puede dar un visor y unas aletas grandes?
  byen meh pwedeh dar oon beesor ee oonas aletas grandes

Q How much will it cost to hire a mask and flippers for an hour?

sound check

j is pronounced like the 'ch' in 'loch':

viaje *byahheh*   pasaje *pasahheh*

q is always followed by **u**, usually as **que** or **qui**. The **u** is then silent:

aquí *akee*   qué *keh*

Practise these words:

raqueta	*rra**ke**ta*	esquiar	*es**kyar***
lejos	***le**hhos*	jugar	*hhoo**gar***

try it out

leisure time

Pair the words in columns A and B to make up names of leisure activities.

A	**B**
bucear	al tenis
montar	en el mar
jugar	en las montañas
hacer	con esnórkel
esquiar	a caballo
pescar	caminatas

mix and match

Match the questions (1–5) and the answers (a–e).

1 ¿Hay algo para niños?
2 ¿Qué hay para ver aquí?
3 ¿Le gusta la salsa?
4 ¿A qué hora empieza el partido?
5 ¿Hay entradas para el concierto?

a Perdone, están agotadas.
b No, no me gusta.
c A las ocho de la noche.
d Sí, hay una feria de diversiones.
e Hay unas ruinas muy interesantes.

as if you were there

Following the prompts, find out what there is for you and your children to do in the sunshine.

(Ask the receptionist if there's anything for children to do here)
Sí, hay un golfito.
(Ask if he has a plan of the town)
Sí. El golfito está aquí.
(Ask where you can play tennis)
Aquí, en el hotel. ¿Quiere alquilar una raqueta?
(Say yes, and thank him. Ask how much it'll cost)
Cinco dólares, todo incluido.

linkup

<table>
<tr><td>¿Hay cancha de tenis?</td><td>Is there a tennis court?</td></tr>
<tr><td>¿Le gusta montar a caballo?</td><td>Do you like horse riding?</td></tr>
<tr><td>No me gustan los toros.</td><td>I don't like bullfighting.</td></tr>
<tr><td>Me gusta pescar.</td><td>I like fishing.</td></tr>
<tr><td>¿Dónde se puede bucear?</td><td>Where can you scuba dive?</td></tr>
<tr><td>¿A qué hora empieza/ termina?</td><td>What time does it start/ finish?</td></tr>
</table>

key phrases

Entertainment

likes, dislikes and preferences

For likes and dislikes, Spanish uses the idea of 'pleasing'.

Me gusta la fotografía. I like photography.
(Literally, 'Photography pleases me'.)

So, for dislikes you say:

No me gusta la salsa. I don't like salsa.

And when what you like is plural, you say:

Me gustan las películas cubanas. I like Cuban films.

You can show preferences very simply:

Me gusta el cine, pero prefiero el teatro. I like the cinema but I prefer the theatre.

And you can express stronger feelings:

Me gusta mucho. I like it a lot.
Me encanta el tango. I adore tango.
No me gusta nada. I don't like it at all.

To say what you like doing, use me gusta followed by the infinitive (dictionary form) of the verb:

Me gusta jugar al fútbol. I like playing football.
No me gusta bailar. I don't like dancing.

can and can't

If you want to find out what you can and can't do in a place, there's a very simple formula:

¿**Se puede** pescar aquí? **Can you** go fishing here?

This is a form of the verb **poder**, but it's best remembered as a very handy little phrase, as in these examples:

¿**Se puede** nadar en el río?
Can you swim in the river?

No se puede estacionar en la plaza.
You can't park in the square.

Emergencies

reporting crime

Report any crime to the police (try the tourist police force first if there is one) and to your embassy. Make sure that the incident is properly recorded and official documents stamped.

In most countries you are required to carry some form of ID.

medical treatment

Ask your doctor which vaccinations are required and try to have them at least six weeks before departure. It is wise to carry Spanish translations of any repeat prescriptions, know your blood group and, if you suffer from a long-term condition such as epilepsy or diabetes, to wear a medical alert bracelet.

Information about local health services is available at tourist offices, and your embassy should also have a list of recommended doctors and clinics.

Medical insurance is essential and for anything serious you should go the best private hospital you can reach. In more remote areas, go to the local health or first aid centre (**centro médico, puesto de**

socorro or **puesto de salud**).

For minor medical problems, head for the chemist's (**farmacia** or **droguería**), usually identified by a green cross. Many medicines are available over the counter without prescription and pharmacists are generally very knowledgeable. Check the expiry date on any medicines you buy.

breakdowns

Beware of small and cheap rental companies; their vehicles may be poorly maintained and an alternative may not be available if you do break down.

Some tour operators offer vehicles with a driver. This can be the safest option since the drivers know the roads, and carry tools and a mobile phone for use in an emergency.

If you have an accident you may have to pay for any damage on the spot and seek reimbursement from the insurance company later. Drivers of vehicles involved in accidents are expected to remain at the scene until the arrival of local police authorities.

post offices

Throughout the region the quickest way of sending mail is to use the main post office in a capital city. Stamps (**estampillas**) can be bought at post offices, hotels and some shops, but post boxes are few and far between.

Always use registered mail (**correo certificado**) for parcels and expect packages to be passed by customs if they are being sent out of the country.

telephones

Public telephone boxes exist but can be unreliable. You can also find public phones in bars and restaurants, although these will often only accept phone cards.

From some of the more remote areas, calls must be made via a central telephone exchange (**la central telefónica**), which is usually found in the main square.

phrasemaker

emergency phrases

you may say ...

Help!	¡Socorro!/¡Auxilio!	*sokorro/owseelyo*
Hello there!	¡Oiga!	*oyga*
Excuse me!	¡Perdón!	*perdon*
Can you help me?	¿Me puede ayudar?	*meh **pwe**deh ayoo**dar***
Where is the nearest ...	¿Dónde está ... más cercana?	***don**deh esta ... mas serka**na***
police station?	la comisaría de policía†	*la komeesa**ree**a deh polee**see**a*
chemist's?	la farmacia	*la far**ma**sya*
petrol station?	la gasolinera/ la estación de servicio†	*la gasolee**ne**ra/la esta**syon** deh ser**bee**syo*
Where is the nearest ...	¿Dónde está ... más cercano?	***don**deh esta ... mas serka**no***
garage?	el taller	*el ta**yer***
hospital?	el hospital	*el ospee**tal***
telephone?	el teléfono	*el te**le**fono*
I need ...	Necesito ...	*nese**see**to*
a doctor.	un doctor.	*oon dok**tor***
an ambulance.	una ambulancia.	***oo**na amboo**lan**sya*
a dentist.	un dentista.	*oon den**tees**ta*
It's an emergency.	Es una emergencia.	*es **oo**na emer**hhen**sya*
Do you speak English?	¿Habla usted inglés?	*abla oos**teth** een**gles***
Leave me alone!	¡Déjeme en paz!	***de**hhemeh en pas*
I'll call the police!	¡Voy a llamar a la policía!	*boy a ya**mar** a la polee**see**a*

Emergencies

describing your symptoms

you may say ...

I'd like an appointment.	Quisiera una cita.	*keesyera oona seeta*
It hurts here.	Me duele aquí.	*meh dweleh akee*
My ... hurts.	Me duele ...	*meh dweleh*
back	la espalda.	*la espalda*
stomach	el estómago.	*el estomago*
head	la cabeza.	*la kabesa*
My ... hurt (a lot).	Me duelen (mucho) ...	*meh dwelen (mootcho)*
shoulders	los hombros.	*los ombros*
kidneys	los riñones.	*los reenyones*
It hurts a little.	Me duele un poco.	*meh dweleh oon poko*
I have toothache. (back/front teeth)	Tengo dolor de muela/diente.	*tengo dolor deh mwela/dyenteh*
My son/daughter has ...	Mi hijo/hija tiene ...	*mee eehho/eehha tyeneh*
earache.	dolor de oído.	*dolor deh oeedo*
a sore throat.	dolor de garganta.	*dolor deh garganta*
I can't move my ...	No puedo mover ...	*no pwedo mober*
toes.	los dedos del pie.	*los dedos del pyeh*
arm.	el brazo.	*el braso*
I fell.	Me caí.	*meh kaee*
I feel sick/shivery.	Tengo nauseas/escalofríos.	*tengo nowseas/eskalofreeos*
I've been sick.	Vomité.	*bomeeteh*
I feel faint.	Estoy mareado/a.	*estoy mareado/a*
I'm ...	Estoy ...	*estoy*
constipated.	estreñido/a.	*estrenyeedo/a*
dehydrated.	deshidratado/a.	*deseedratado/a*
I have ...	Tengo ...	*tengo*
diarrhoea.	diarrea.	*dyarrea*
a bad hangover.	una resaca/una cruda† terrible.	*oona rresaka/oona krooda terreebleh*

He/She has ...	Tiene ...	*tyeneh*
a fever.	fiebre/calentura.	*fyebreh/kalentoora*
asthma.	asma.	*asma*
I've cut/burnt myself.	Me corté/quemé.	*meh korteh/kemeh*
I've lost a filling.	Se me cayó un empaste†	*seh meh kayo oon empasteh*
I'm allergic to penicillin.	Soy alérgico/a a la penicilina.	*soy alerhheeko/a a la peneeseeleena*
I'm ...	Soy ...	*soy*
diabetic.	diabético/a.	*dyabeteeko/a*
HIV positive.	seropositivo/a.	*sero-poseeteebo/a*
I'm pregnant.	Estoy embarazada/en estado.	*estoy embarasada/en estado*
Can I have a receipt for my insurance?	¿Me puede dar un recibo para el seguro?	*meh pwedeh dar oon rreseebo para el segooro*

you may hear ...

¿Dónde le duele?	*dondeh leh dweleh*	Where does it hurt?
¿Le duele mucho?	*leh dweleh mootcho*	Does it hurt a lot?
Necesito examinarlo/la.	*neseseeto eksameenarlo/la*	I need to examine you.
No es nada grave.	*no es nada grabeh*	It's nothing serious.
Tiene ...	*tyeneh*	You've got
una intoxicación.	*oona eentokseekasyon*	food poisoning.
una infección.	*oona eenfeksyon*	an infection.
la gripe.	*la greepeh*	the flu.
¿Está vacunado/a contra ...	*esta bacoonado/la kontra*	Have you been vaccinated against ...
el tétano?	*el tetano*	tetanus?
la tifoidea?	*la teefoydea*	typhoid?
¿Está tomando algún medicamento?	*esta tomando algoon medeekamento*	Are you on any medication?
¿Es alérgico/a a algo?	*es alerhheeko/a a algo*	Are you allergic to anything?
Tiene el pie roto.	*tyeneh el pyeh rroto*	You've broken your foot.

Tiene la pierna rota.	*tyeneh la pyerna rrota*	You've broken your leg.
Tiene un esguince en la rodilla/el tobillo.	*tyeneh oon esgeenseh en la rrodeeya/el tobeeyo*	He/She has a sprained knee/ankle.

Tiene una fractura en ...
   la muñeca.
   el dedo.
	tyeneh oona fraktoora en
	   la moonyeka
	   el dedo
		He/She has a fractured ...
		   wrist.
		   finger/toe.

Le voy a recetar unos antibióticos/unas pastillas.	*leh boy a resetar oonos anteebyoteekos/oonas pasteeyas*	I'm going to prescribe some antibiotics/tablets.
Tome mucha agua.	*tomeh mootcha agwa*	Drink lots of water.
No se ponga al sol.	*no seh ponga al sol*	Stay out of the sun.
Debe descansar/dormir.	*debeh deskansar/dormeer*	You must rest/sleep.

No debe ...
   levantarse.
   hacer ejercicio.
	no debeh
	   lebantarseh
	   aser ehherseesyo
		You mustn't ...
		   get up.
		   exercise.

check out 1

You go to see the doctor about a stomach problem.

○ Me duele el estómago.
 meh dweleh el estomago

– ¿Está estreñida?
 esta estrenyeeda

○ No, tengo diarrea.
 no tengo dyarrea

– Le voy a recetar unas pastillas. Tómelas cada ocho horas. Y tome mucha agua.
 leh boy a resetar oonas pasteeyas. tomelas kada otcho oras. ee tomeh mootcha agwa

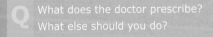
What does the doctor prescribe?
What else should you do?

parts of the body

breasts	los senos	*los senos*
chest	el pecho	*el petcho*
chin	el mentón/la barbilla†	*el menton/la barbeeya*
ear (inner/outer)	el oído/la oreja	*el oeedo/la orehha*
elbow	el codo	*el kodo*
eyes	los ojos	*los ohhos*
hand	la mano	*la mano*
heart	el corazón	*el korason*
hip	la cadera	*la kadera*
liver	el hígado	*el eegado*
lungs	los pulmones	*los poolmones*
neck	el cuello	*el kweyo*
mouth	la boca	*la boka*
nose	la nariz	*la narees*
ribs	las costillas	*las kosteeyas*
spine	la columna	*la koloomna*
thigh	el muslo	*el mooslo*
thumb	el pulgar	*el poolgar*

at the chemist's
you may say …

Do you have anything for …	¿Tiene algo para …	*tyeneh algo para*
bites?	las picaduras?	*las peekadooras*
sunburn?	las quemaduras del sol?	*las kemadooras del sol*
sunstroke?	la insolación?	*la eensolasyon*
travel sickness?	el mareo?	*el mareo*
I've got …	Tengo …	*tengo*
a cough	tos.	*tos*
a rash	un salpullido.	*oon salpooyeedo*
an upset stomach	un malestar estomacal.	*oon malestar estomakal*
I've got a cold.	Tengo un resfriado.	*tengo oon resfryado*

Emergencies

Do you have ...?	¿Tiene ...	tyeneh
aspirin	aspirina?	aspeereena
contact lens solution	líquido para lentes de contacto?	leekeedo para lentes de kontakto
plasters	curitas?	kooreetas
Does it have side effects?	¿Tiene contraindicaciones/ efectos secundarios?	tyeneh kontra-eendeekasyones/ efektos sekoondaryos
I need some ...	Necesito ...	neseseeto
condoms	condones/ preservativos	kondones/ preserbateebos
painkillers	calmantes/ analgésicos	kalmantes/ analhheseekos
antihistamine	un antihistamínico	oon anteestameeneeko
(strong) insect repellent	un repelente de insectos (fuerte)	oon repelenteh deh eensektos (fwerteh)
Do you sell ...	¿Tienen ...	tyenen
nappies?	pañales?	panyales
baby food?	comida para bebés?	komeeda para bebes
sun cream/block?	la crema anti solar/ el bloqueador solar?	la krema antee-solar/ el blokeador solar
aftersun lotion?	la crema para después del sol/la crema post solar?	la krema para despwes del sol/la krema post solar
sanitary towels?	las toallas higiénicas/ sanitarias?	las twayas eehhyeneekas/ saneetaryas
tampons?	los tampones?	los tampones

you may hear ...

¿Qué comió/bebió?	keh komyo/bebyo	What have you eaten/drunk?
¿Qué síntomas tiene?	keh seentomas tyeneh	What symptoms do you have?
Póngase esta pomada/crema enseguida.	pongaseh esta pomada/krema ensegeeda	Put this cream on straight away.

una cucharadita de jarabe	oona kootcharadeeta deh hharabeh	one teaspoonful of syrup
Tome esta medicina/este remedio ...	tomeh esta medeeseena/esteh remedyo	Take this medicine ...
una vez al día.	oona bes al deea	once a day.
dos/tres veces al día.	dos/tres beses al deea	twice/three times a day.
antes/después de las comidas.	antes/despwes deh las komeedas	before/after meals.
cada (cuatro) horas.	kada (kwatro) oras	every (four) hours.
Puede causar somnolencia.	pwedeh kowsar somnolensya	It may cause drowsiness.

check out 2

You have sunburn and seek advice at the chemist's.

○ ¿Tiene algo para las quemaduras del sol?
tyeneh algo para las kemadooras del sol

– ¿Le duele mucho?
leh dweleh mootcho

○ Sí, los hombros y la espalda.
see los ombros ee la espalda

– Póngase esta crema tres veces al día. Y no se ponga al sol.
pongaseh esta krema tres beses al deea. ee no seh ponga al sol

○ Gracias. ¿Cuánto le debo?
grasyas. kwanto leh debo

(¿Cuánto le debo? = What do I owe you?)

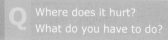

Q Where does it hurt?
What do you have to do?

car breakdown

you may say ...

I've broken down.	El coche se me dañó.[1]	*el kotcheh seh meh danyo*
The car has a flat tyre.	Se me ponchó una llanta.[2]	*seh meh pontcho oona yanta*

The ... isn't working.
  engine
  brake
	El ... no sirve.
	  motor
	  freno
		*el ... no seerbeh
		  motor
		  freno*

... aren't working.
  The windscreen wipers
 	
  The locks
	... no sirven.
	  Los limpiadores
	
	  Los seguros
		*... no seerben
		  los leempyadores
		
		  los segooros*

I've run out of petrol.	No tengo gasolina†.	*no tengo gasoleena*
The car won't start.	El coche no arranca.	*el kotcheh no arranka*
The battery is flat.	La batería está baja.	*la batereea esta bahha*
Can you send a mechanic?	¿Puede mandarme un mecánico?	*pwedeh mandarmeh oon mekaneeko*
I'm on the highway/ road to ...	Estoy en la autopista/la carretera† a ...	*estoy en la owto-peestal/la karretera a*

I'm ...
  at kilometre 110
 	
  near to ...
  (15) kilometres from ...
	Estoy ...
	  en el kilómetro ciento diez
	  cerca de ...
	  a (quince) kilómetros de ...
		*estoy
		  en el keelometro syento dyes
		  serka deh
		  a (keenseh) keelometros deh*

How long will it take?	¿Cuánto tomará?	*kwanto tomara*
When will it be ready?	¿Cuándo estará listo?	*kwando estara leesto*

[1]Mexico: El coche se me descompuso. *el kotcheh seh meh deskompooso* Argentina: El auto se me rompió. *el owto seh meh rrompyo* Chile: El auto cayó en pana. *el owto kayo en pana* Colombia: El carro se me varó. *el karro seh meh baro*

[2]Argentina: Se me pinchó una rueda. *seh meh peentcho oona rweda*

¿Qué le pasa?	*keh leh pasa*	What's the matter?
¿Cuál es su número de placa†?	*kwal es soo noomero deh plaka*	What's your registration number?
¿En dónde está?	*en donde esta*	Where are you?
Le mandamos un mecánico …	*leh mandamos oon mekaneeko*	We'll send a mechanic …
ahorita/enseguida/ ya mismo	*aoreeta/ensegeeda/ ya meesmo*	immediately.
en dos horas.	*en dos oras*	in two hours.

reporting crime

you may say …

I've lost my …	Perdí …	*perdee*
wallet.	la cartera/la billetera.	*la kartera/la beeyetera*
laptop.	la computadora portátil.	*la kompootadora portateel*
I've had my … stolen.	Me robaron …	*meh rrobaron*
suitcase	la maleta†.	*la maleta*
handbag	la bolsa/la cartera.	*la bolsa/la kartera*
camera	la cámara.	*la kamara*
My car has been broken into.	Me abrieron el coche para robar.	*meh abryeron el kotcheh para rrobar*
I was mugged.	Me atracaron.	*meh atrakaron*
I had an accident …	Tuve un accidente …	*toobeh oon akseedenteh*
this morning.	esta mañana.	*esta manyana*
yesterday afternoon.	ayer en la tarde.	*ayer en la tardeh*
… ago	hace …	*aseh*
five minutes	cinco minutos	*seenko meenootos*
one hour	una hora	*oona ora*
in the street/a shop	en la calle/una tienda†	*en la kayeh/oona tyenda*

I think	Creo	*kreo*
I don't know.	No sé.	*no seh*
It was ...	Era ...	*era*
big.	grande.	*grandeh*
blue.	azul.	*asool*
made of leather.	de cuero/piel.	*deh kwero/pyel*

you may hear ...

¿Cuándo/Dónde fue el robo?	*kwando/dondeh fwe el rrobo*	When/Where was the robbery?
¿Está herido/a?	*esta ereedo/a*	Are you hurt?
¿Qué traía en la bolsa?	*keh traeea en la bolsa*	What did you have in your bag?
¿Cómo era?	*komo era*	What was it like?
¿Nombre?	*nombreh*	Name?
Su pasaporte, por favor.	*soo pasaporteh por fabor*	Your passport, please.
¿Sabe su número de pasaporte?	*sabeh soo noomero deh pasaporteh*	Do you know your passport number?

valuables

100 pesos in ...	cien pesos en ...	*syen pesos en*
cash	efectivo	*efekteebo*
travellers' cheques	cheques de viaje	*tchekes deh byahheh*
bank cards	las tarjetas del banco	*las tarhhetas del banko*
briefcase	el portafolio/el maletín	*el portafolyo/el maleteen*
driving licence	la licencia de manejar†	*la leesensya deh manehhar*
jewellery	las joyas	*las hhoyas*
keys	las llaves	*las yabes*
mobile phone	el celular	*el seloolar*
money	la plata/el dinero	*la plata/el deenero*
MP3 player	el mp3	*el emeh peh tres*
purse	el monedero	*el monedero*
tickets	los pasajes	*los pasahhes*
watch	el reloj	*el rrelohh*

check out 3

You report a robbery at a police station.

○ ¡Me robaron la bolsa!
*meh ro***bar***on la* ***bol****sa*

– ¿Cuándo fue el robo?
kwan*do fwe el* ***rro****bo*

○ Hace media hora, en el cine.
*a*seh ***me****dya* ***o****ra en el* ***see****neh*

– ¿Qué traía en la bolsa?
*keh tra***ee***a en la* ***bol****sa*

○ Dinero, y mi pasaporte.
*dee***ne****ro ee mee pasa***por***teh*

– ¿Sabe su número de pasaporte?
sa*beh soo* ***noo****mero deh pasa***por***teh*

○ No sé.
no seh

 Q What did the police officer want to know first?
What number did he ask about?

sound check

The letter **c** in Spanish has two different pronunciations depending on its position in a word.

In Latin American Spanish, when **c** is followed by the letter **e** or **i** it is pronounced like the 's' in 'see':

cercano *ser**ka**no*   emergencia *emer**hhen**sya*

In all other positions, **c** is pronounced like the 'k' in 'kit':

comisaría *komeesa**ree**a*   doctor *dok**tor***

Practise with these words:

cabeza *ka**be**sa*   alérgico *a**ler**hheeko*
ambulancia *amboo**lan**sya*   recetar *rese**tar***

126

try it out

word search

Find the names of the following body parts:

chest
eye
knee
head
neck
back

C	A	B	E	Z	A	F	H
D	E	D	S	C	O	D	R
I	B	I	P	E	C	H	O
A	O	E	A	C	U	M	C
F	C	N	L	U	E	A	R
R	R	O	D	I	L	L	A
A	J	T	A	S	L	E	Z
F	R	E	N	T	O	J	O

health concerns

Match the diagnosis with its symptoms and likely prescription. Each symptom might be characteristic of more than one illness, and each of the complaints might have more than one symptom and prescription.

Diagnosis	**Symptom**	**Prescription**
infección	diarrea	analgésico
insolación	dolor de cabeza	antibiótico
gripe	escalofríos	pastillas
	calentura	crema
	náuseas	jarabe

as if you were there

Follow the prompts to play your part at the doctor's surgery.

Buenos días, ¿qué le pasa?
(Say you have food poisoning)
¿Qué síntomas tiene?
(Say that you've been sick)
¿Tiene diarrea también?
(Say yes, that you also have diarrhoea)
Tome estas pastillas cuatro veces al día.
(Thank him and say goodbye)

(también = also)

linkup

key phrases		
	¿Me puede ayudar?	**Can you** help **me?**
	Necesito un dentista.	**I need** a dentist.
	Tengo asma.	**I have** asthma.
	Me duele la espalda.	**My** back **hurts.**
	¿Tiene algo para la gripe?	**Do you have anything for** the flu?
	Perdí mis llaves.	**I lost** my keys.
	Me robaron la cámara.	**I had** my camera **stolen.**

There are two simple ways of saying what's hurting. You can say:

Tengo dolor de estómago. I have stomach ache
(literally, 'I have pain of the stomach').

Or you can use **me duele**, which you use in the same way as **me gusta**:

Me duele el estómago. My stomach hurts
(literally, 'it hurts to me the stomach').

Me duelen los oídos. My ears hurt
(literally, 'they hurt to me the ears').

possession

The apostrophe s ('s and s') doesn't exist in Spanish, so to express possession or belonging, you change the order of the words:

El apartamento de mi amigo. My friend's flat
(literally, 'the apartment of my friend').

El coche de mi hermana. My sister's car.

La casa de mis vecinos. My neighbours' house.

The word **de** is also very useful when linking two other words:

Un dolor de cabeza. A headache.

Una bolsa de cuero. A leather bag.

La capital de Perú. Peru's capital.

For more on possession, see the Language Builder, p135.

gender

All Spanish nouns (words for people, things and concepts) are either masculine or feminine. The gender of a word affects the form of 'a' and 'the' used before it, and any adjectives (describing words such as 'big', 'small') used with it.

Masculine words usually end in **-o**: teléfono, sombrero (telephone, hat).

Feminine words usually end in **-a**: farmacia, casa (chemist's, house).

Words ending in other letters can be either masculine or feminine: you just have to learn them as you go along: tomate and hotel are masculine; miel (honey) and calle (street) are feminine.

'a' & 'the': the articles

	masculine	feminine	masc. plural	fem. plural
a, some	un	una	unos	unas
the	el	la	los	las

Some examples:

una cerveza a beer   un vaso a glass
la camisa the shirt   el vestido the dress
las camisas the shirts   los vestidos the dresses

When learning a new word, it's easier to remember its gender if you learn it with an article. So, for example, instead of just learning the words cereza (cherry) and melón (melon), learn una/la cereza, and un/el melón.

singular & plural

To talk about more than one person or thing, you normally add an **-s** to the word if it ends in a vowel and **-es** if it ends in a consonant:

una pera one pear	dos pera**s** two pears
un plátano one banana	dos plátano**s** two bananas
un señor one gentleman	dos señor**es** two gentlemen
un limón one lemon	dos limon**es** two lemons

adjectives

Adjectives 'agree' with the nouns they describe, so they have different endings for masculine and feminine, singular and plural words. Often adjectives end in **-o** for masculine or **-a** for feminine, and add an **-s** for the plural of both.

singular

un museo modern**o** a modern museum
una iglesia modern**a** a modern church

plural

manzanas amarill**as** yellow apples (manzana is feminine)
pimientos amarill**os** yellow peppers (pimiento is masculine)

Some adjectives, including those ending in **-e** and most of those ending in a consonant, only have one singular form, and add an **-s** or an **-es** in the plural:
una manzana verd**e**, manzanas verd**es**
a green apple, green apples
un pimiento verd**e**, pimientos verd**es**
a green pepper, green peppers
una camisa azu**l**, camisas azul**es** a blue shirt, blue shirts
un coche azu**l**, coches azul**es** a blue car, blue cars

As you can see, in Spanish adjectives generally come after the noun. There are some common exceptions which always come before the noun:

alguno (any, some)	cada (every, all)
mucho (much, many)	otro (other)
poco (not much, few)	todo (every, all)
último (last)	

verbs

The endings of Spanish verbs change according to who does the action and when. Look at the example for the verb hablar (to speak), below. These endings are for regular verbs ending in **-ar**.

(For the different meanings of 'you', see 'talking to people', on the next page.)

hablar: to speak	
(yo) hablo	I speak
(tú) hablas	you speak
(él/ella; usted) habla	he/she/it speaks; you speak
(nosotros) hablamos	we speak
(ellos/ellas; ustedes) hablan	they speak; you speak

There are two other common patterns of verbs: those ending in **-er** and those ending in **-ir**. The following examples show the endings of regular verbs of these types.

comer: to eat	
(yo) como	I eat
(tú) comes	you eat
(él/ella; usted) come	he/she/it eats; you eat
(nosotros) comemos	we eat
(ellos/ellas; ustedes) comen	they eat; you eat

vivir: to live	
(yo) vivo	I live
(tú) vives	you live
(él/ella; usted) vive	he/she/it lives; you live
(nosotros) vivimos	we live
(ellos/ellas; ustedes) viven	they live; you live

Verbs that follow the patterns above are called regular verbs. However, many of the common verbs are irregular verbs and must be learnt individually.

Language **Builder**

talking to people

In Spanish you use a different word for 'you' depending on how many people you are talking to and how well you know them.

For example, you use:
usted to someone you don't know well or an older person (formal)
tú or vos to a friend, member of the family, or younger person (informal) (vos is a Latin American regional variation, particularly common in Argentina and Uruguay).

This also affects the form of the verb you use, so, for example, here are different ways you would ask 'How are you?' in Latin American Spanish:
¿Cómo está (usted)?
To an adult you have not met before or know only a little.
¿Cómo estás (tú or vos)?
To a child or to an adult you are friendly with.
¿Cómo están (ustedes)?
To more than one person, whether you have just met them or are friendly with them.

If in doubt, it is always safer to be polite and use the formal form (usted or ustedes).

pronouns

In Spanish you don't generally need to use a pronoun (I, you, he etc.) with the verb, as the ending of the verb makes it clear who is being referred to.

Hablo inglés. I speak English. (instead of Yo hablo inglés.)
¿Tiene aceite? Do you have any oil? (instead of ¿Tiene usted aceite?)

the two verbs 'to be'

There are two verbs meaning 'to be' in Spanish, which can be quite confusing. They are ser and estar.

Estar is used for locations and to describe the condition or state (often temporary) that someone or something is in. For example:

¿Dónde está la Plaza Mayor? Where is the Main Square?
Está al final de la calle. It's at the end of the street.
Está enfermo. He is ill.

Otherwise ser is used:

¿Cómo es la plaza mayor? What is the main square like?
Es magnífica. It's magnificent.
Soy inglés. I am English.

They are both irregular:

	ser	estar
yo	soy	estoy
tú	eres	estás
él/ella/usted	es	está
nosotros/as	somos	estamos
ellos/as/ustedes	son	están

questions

There are two easy ways to ask a question. You can change the word order of a statement:

El mercado está cerca. The market is close.
¿Está cerca el mercado? Is the market close?

Or you can use the same order, but with a question intonation:

Tiene manzanas. You have some apples.
¿Tiene manzanas? Do you have any apples?

The rise in your voice turns the sentence into a question, and the context in which you are speaking will usually prevent any confusion.

Some useful question words:

¿**Dónde** está la catedral? **Where** is the cathedral?
¿**Cuánto** cuesta? **How much** does it cost?
¿**Quién** vive aquí? **Who** lives here?
¿**Qué** color prefieres? **Which** colour do you prefer?
¿**Por qué** haces eso? **Why** are you doing that?
¿**Cuándo** empieza la película? **When** does the film begin?
¿A **qué** hora termina? **What** time does it finish?

talking about possession

De (of) is used to show possession:
la maleta de Anna Anna's suitcase

There are special words for personal possession. They are adjectives (see above), so they all 'agree' with the nouns they refer to:

mi reloj my watch
mis gafas my glasses

	singular	plural
my	mi	mis
your (formal)	su	sus
your (informal)	tu	tus
his/her/its	su	sus
our	nuestro/a	nuestros/as
their/your plural	su	sus

this, that, these, those

These words behave like adjectives so they have different forms, depending on what they refer to:

este melón/estos melones this melon/these melons
esta sandía/estas sandías this watermelon/these watermelons
ese melón/esos melones that melon/those melons
esa sandía/esas sandías that watermelon/those watermelons

things you like: gustar

To talk about what you like and dislike in Spanish, use the phrases me gusta and me gustan:

Me gusta el vino tinto, no me gusta el vino blanco. I like red wine, I don't like white wine.
Me gustan las alcachofas, no me gustan las berenjenas. I like artichokes, I don't like aubergines.

What the Spanish literally means is 'Red wine is pleasing to me.' and 'Artichokes are pleasing to me.'. So, when you are talking about one thing, use the singular form me gusta, and when you are talking about more than one thing, use the plural form me gustan. Try to remember that the verb gustar means 'to please', and take it from there.

Answers

Bare Necessities .....

check out
1 his wife; have a good day/time
2 about 1,000 pesos; your passport

missing vowels
cuatro; ocho; diez; dieciséis; veinte; cincuenta; noventa; cien; trescientos; mil

get it right
1 ¿Hay baños?
2 Buenas noches.
3 ¡Salud!
4 Con permiso.
5 ¿Cuánto cuestan los aretes?
6 ¿Hay ascensor/elevador?
7 Perdón/Perdone.

as if you were there
Más despacio, por favor.
mas despasyo por fabor
Sí.
see
Soy inglesa.
soy eenglesa
¿Cómo?
komo
Me llamo Anna.
meh yamo anna

Getting Around ....

check out
1 no, it's two blocks away
2 2,060 pesos
3 true
4 every hour; six hours

find the right place
1 una casa de cambio/un banco

2 un café internet/un cibercafé
3 la estación de trenes
4 un cajero automático
5 la oficina de turismo
6 una parada de (auto)buses
7 una gasolinera/una estación de servicio

mix and match
1 e; 2 d; 3 b; 4 a; 5 c

as if you were there
¿Pasa por Bellas Artes?
pasa por beyas artes
¿Cuánto es a Bellas Artes?
kwanto es a beyas artes
¿Me puede decir dónde bajarme?
meh pwedeh deseer donde bahharmeh
Gracias.
grasyas

Somewhere to Stay ...

check out
1 one; 400 pesos
2 true; false
3 true; true

'a' puzzle
1 habitación 2 llave 3 ascensor
4 baño 5 desayuno

as if you were there
No hay jabón.
no iy hhabon
Veintiséis. ¿Cómo funciona la ducha?
baynteesays. komo foonsyona la dootcha

Buying Things ....

1 because they don't have any; 24 pesos
2 100 pesos; some earrings
3 no

food mixer

jamón; melón; cebolla; queso; huevos; naranja; leche; lechuga

phrase matcher

1 c; 2 e; 3 a; 4 b; 5 d

as if you were there

Me gusta. ¿Cuánto cuesta?
*meh **goo**sta. **kwan**to **kwes**ta*
¿Se aceptan tarjetas de crédito?
*seh a**sep**tan tar**hhe**tas deh **kre**deeto*
¿Es el último precio?
*es el **ool**teemo **pre**syo*
Me lo llevo.
*meh lo **ye**bo*

Café Life ....

check out
1 chicken, ham and vegetarian
2 because they didn't have any sparkling water
3 chocolate

crossword

1 caramelo	4 vainilla
2 mora	5 melón
3 limón	

split the difference

1 g; 2 h; 3 a; 4 b; 5 f; 6 c; 7 d; 8 i; 9 e

empanada and jamón are not drinks

as if you were there

Buenas tardes. (Quisiera/me puede dar) un té con leche. ¿Qué refrescos tiene?
***bwe**nas **tar**des. (kee**sye**ra/meh **pwe**deh dar) oon teh kon **le**tcheh. keh re**fres**kos **tye**ne*
Una limonada, por favor.
oo**na leemo**na**da por fa**bor
Dos empanadas, por favor.
*dos empa**na**das por fa**bor***
Unas papas fritas.
***oo**nas **pa**pas **free**tas*

Eating Out ....

check out

1 true; false
2 fish, tomatoes, onion, chillies and olives
3 because you are allergic to shellfish; no

get it right

a Tenemos una reservación a nombre de [your name/ surname].
b ¿Tiene una silla para niños?
c ¿Pica mucho?
d Soy alérgico/a a los lácteos.
e Esto no es lo que pedí.
f ¿Me puede traer más pan, por favor?

on the menu

Menu 3 is the best option; Menu 1 has fish and Menu 2 has shellfish and nuts.

as if you were there

Buenas noches. Una mesa para dos.

bwenas notches. oona mesa para dos

Una botella de vino tinto y unos tacos de pollo, por favor.

oona boteya deh beeno teento ee oonos takos deh poyo por fabor

¿Es agua purificada?

es agwa pooreefeekada

Entertainment ....

check out

1 every day
2 7.00am; here (at the hotel)
3 40 pesos

leisure time

bucear con esnórkel; montar a caballo; jugar al tenis; hacer caminatas; esquiar en las montañas; pescar en el mar

mix and match

1 d; 2 e; 3 b; 4 c; 5 a

as if you were there

¿Hay algo para niños aquí?

iy algo para neenyos akee

¿Tiene un plano de la ciudad?

tyeneh oon plano deh la syoodath

¿Dónde se puede jugar al tenis?

dondeh seh pwedeh hhoogar al tenees

Sí, gracias. ¿Cuánto cuesta?

see grasyas. kwanto kwesta

Emergencies ....

check out

1 some pills; drink a lot of water
2 your shoulders and back; apply the cream three times a day and stay out of the sun
3 when the robbery had taken place; passport number

word search

C	A	B	E	Z	A	F	H
D	E	D	S	C	O	D	R
I	B	I	P	E	C	H	O
A	O	E	A	C	U	M	C
F	C	N	L	U	E	A	R
R	R	O	D	I	L	L	A
A	J	T	A	S	L	E	Z
F	R	E	N	T	O	J	O

health concerns

Infección: diarrea, náuseas, dolor de cabeza; crema, pastillas, antibiótico

Insolación: dolor de cabeza, escalofríos, náuseas, calentura; pastillas, analgésico

Gripe: dolor de cabeza, escalofríos; analgésico, jarabe, pastillas

as if you were there

Tengo una intoxicación

tengo oona eentokseekasyon

Vomité.

bomeeteh

Sí, también tengo diarrea.

see tambyen tengo dyarrea

Gracias y adiós.

grasyas ee adyos

(f) = feminine, (inf) = informal
(And) = Andean Region,
(Arg) = Argentina (Bol) = Bolivia, (Carib)
= Caribbean, (CAm) = Central America,
(Chi) = Chile, (Col) = Colombia,
(Cub) = Cuba, (Ecu) = Ecuador, (Mex)
= Mexico, (Per) = Peru, (PtR) = Puerto
Rico, (SCon) = Southern Cone,
(Uru) = Uruguay, (Ven) = Venezuela

A

a little un poco *oon poko*
a lot mucho/a *mootcho/a*
about de; sobre *deh; sobreh*
abseiling descenso en rapel, el *desenso en rrapel*
to accept aceptar *aseptar*
accident accidente, el *akseedenteh*
ache dolor, el *dolor*
adult adulto/a *adoolto/a*
aeroplane avión, el *abyon*
after después *despwes*
aftersun lotion crema para después del sol, la; crema post solar, la *krema para despwes del sol; krema post solar*
afternoon tarde, la *tardeh*
(two hours) ago hace (dos horas) *ase (dos oras)*
air conditioned aire acondicionado/a *iyreh akondeesyonado/a*
airport aeropuerto, el *aeropwerto*
all todo/a(s) *todo/a(s)*
allergic alérgico/a *alerhheeko/a*
alone; neat solo/a *solo/a*
also también *tambyen*
I am soy *soy*
ambulance ambulancia, la *amboolansya*
antibiotics antibióticos, los *anteebyoteekos*
antihistamine antihistamínico, el *anteestameeneeko*
appointment cita, la *seeta*
architect arquitecto/a *arkeetekto/a*
area zona, la *zona*
to arrive llegar *yegar*
art arte, el *arteh*
art gallery galería de arte, la *galereea deh arteh*
aspirin aspirina, la *aspeereena*
asthma asma, el *asma*
to attack asaltar *asaltar*

B

B&B albergue, el *albergeh*
bad malo/a *malo/a*
bag bolsa, la *bolsa*
  hand/shoulder bolso, el; cartera, la *bolso; kartera*

sleeping bag bolsa de dormir, la *bolsa deh dormeer*
ball pelota, la *pelota*
banana plátano, el; banano, el; banana, la; (Carib) guineo, el; (Ven) cambúr, el *platano; banano; banana; geeneo; kamboor*
bank banco, el *banko*
bar bar, el; cantina, la *bar; kanteena*
basket canasta, la *kanasta*
battery pila, la *peela;* (car) batería, la *batereea*
to be estar; ser *estar; ser*
beach playa, la *playa*
bean frijol, el; poroto, el; (Carib) habichuela, la; (Ven) caraota, la *freehhol; poroto; abeetchwela; karaota*
bed cama, la *kama*
  double cama doble, la; cama matrimonial, la *kama dobleh; kama matreemonyal*
  single cama individual, la *kama eendeebeedwal*
before antes *antes*
behind detrás de *detras deh*
to believe creer *kreer*
bend curva, la *koorba*
bicycle bicicleta, la *beeseekleta*
  mountain bicicleta de montaña, la *beeseekleta deh montanya*
big grande *grandeh*
biking ciclismo, el *seekleesmo*
  mountain ciclismo de montaña, el *seekleesmo deh montanya*
bill cuenta, la *kwenta*
bin (rubbish) basurero, el *basoorero*
to bite morder *morder*
black negro/a *negro/a*
blanket cobija, la; (Arg) frazada, la *kobeehha; frasada*
blind persiana, la *persyana*
blue azul *asool*
boarding house pensión, la *pensyon*
boat barco, el *barko*
body cuerpo, el *kwerpo*
bone hueso, el *weso*
bottle botella, la *boteya*
bowl tazón, el *tason*
box caja, la *kahha*
boy muchacho, el; chico, el *mootchatcho; tcheeko*
bra brasier, el; (Arg) corpiño, el; (CAm) sostén, el *brasyer; korpeenyo; sosten*
brakes frenos, los *frenos*
brass latón, el *laton*
bread pan, el *pan*
to break romper *rromper*

to break down dañarse; (Arg) romperse; (Chi) caer en pana; (Col) vararse; (Mex) descomponerse *danyarseh; rromperseh; kaer en pana; bararseh; deskomponerseh*
breakfast desayuno, el *desayoono*
bridge puente, el *pwenteh*
broken roto/a *rrotola*
brown marrón; café *marron; kafeh*
buffet bufé, el *boofeh*
bullfighting corridas de toros, las; toros, los *korreedas deh toros; toros*
bureau de change casa de cambio, la *kasa deh kambyo*
burger hamburguesa, la *amboorgesa*
to burn oneself quemarse *kemarseh*
bus autobús, el; (Arg) colectivo, el; (Carib) guagua, la; (Mex) camión, el *owtoboos; kolekteebo; gwagwa; kamyon*
but pero *pero*
butter mantequilla, la; (Arg) manteca, la *mantekeeya; manteka*
to buy comprar *komprar*

C

café café, el; cafetería, la *kafeh; kafetereea*
cake pastel, el; torta, la *pastel; torta*
to be called llamarse *yamarseh*
camera cámara *kamara*
   digital cámara digital, la *kamara deehheetal*
   disposable cámara desechable, la *kamara desetchableh*
campsite camping, el *kampeen*
car (CAm, And) carro, el; (Mex, Carib) coche, el; (SCon) auto, el *karro; kotcheh; owto*
car park estacionamiento, el *estasyonamyento*
caravan tráiler, el *trayler*
card tarjeta, la *tarhheta*
   credit tarjeta de crédito, la *tarhheta deh kredeeto*
   debit tarjeta de débito, la *tarhheta deh debeeto*
   phone tarjeta telefónica, la *tarhheta telefoneeka*
   student carnet (de estudiante), el *karnet*
carnival carnaval, el *karnabal*
to carry; to take llevar *yebar*
carved tallado/a *tayadola*
cash efectivo, el *efekteebo*
cashpoint cajero automático, el *kaheero owtomateeko*

cassava yuca, la; (Arg) mandioca, la *yooka; mandyoka*
castle castillo, el *kasteeyo*
cathedral catedral, la *katedral*
ceramics cerámica, la *serameeka*
chair silla, la *seeya*
   high silla para niños, la *seeya para neenyos*
to change cambiar *kambyar*
change (money) cambio, el *kambyo*
changing rooms vestidores, los *besteedores*
cheap barato/a *baratola*
to check revisar *rrebeesar*
cheers! ¡salud! *salooth*
cheese queso, el *keso*
chemist's farmacia, la; droguería, la *farmasya; drogereea*
child niño/a, el/la *neenyola*
chin mentón, el; barbilla, la; (Arg) pera, la *menton; barbeeya; pera*
chips; crisps papas fritas, las *papas freetas*
chocolate chocolate, el *tchokolate*
Christmas Navidad, la *nabeedath*
church iglesia, la *eeglesya*
cinema cine, el *seeneh*
city ciudad, la *syudath*
to clean limpiar *leempyar*
cloakroom guardarropa, el *gwarda-rropa*
to close cerrar *serrar*
close (near) cerca *serka*
closed cerrado/a *serradola*
coach station terminal de autobuses, la *terminal deh owtobooses*
coast costa, la *kosta*
coat abrigo, el; (Arg: men's) sobretodo, el; (Arg: women's) tapado, el *abreego; sobretodo; tapado*
coin moneda, la *moneda*
cold frío/a; (medical) resfriado, el *freeo; resfryado*
   I'm cold tengo frío *tengo freeo*
   It's cold hace frío *aseh freeo*
   I've got a cold tengo un resfriado *tengo oon resfryado*
to come in entrar *entrar*
concert concierto, el *konsyerto*
conditioner acondicionador, el; bálsamo, el *akondeesyonador; balsamo*
condom condón, el; preservativo, el *kondon; preserbateebo*
constipated estreñido/a *estrenyeedola*
contact lens solution líquido para lentes de contacto, el *leekeedo para lentes deh kontakto*
to contain contener *kontener*

cooker estufa, la; cocina, la *estoofa; koseena*
copper cobre, el *kobreh*
corn maíz, el *maees*
  on the cob mazorca, la; maíz, el; (Mex) elote, el; (SCon) choclo, el *masorka; maees; eloteh; tchoklo*
corner esquina, la *eskeena*
cot cuna, la *koona*
cotton algodón, el *algodon*
cough tos, la *tos*
cough mixture jarabe para la tos, el *hharabeh para la tos*
course (food) plato, el *plato*
  main plato principal, el *plato preenseepal*
cream (food) crema, la; (ointment) pomada, la; crema, la *krema; pomada; krema*
  shaving crema de afeitar, la *krema deh afaytar*
to cross cruzar *kroosar*
crossroads cruce de caminos, el; intersección de vías, la *krooseh deh kameenos; eenterseksyon deh beeas*
cup taza, la; (Col, Per) pocillo, el *tasa; poseeyo*
current adaptor adaptador de corriente, el *adaptador deh korryenteh*
to cut oneself cortarse *kortarseh*

D

dairy lácteos, los *lakteos*
danger peligro *peleegro*
dangerous peligroso/a *peleegroso*
daughter hija, la *eehha*
day día, el *deea*
dehydrated deshidratado/a *deseedratado/a*
delicious rico/a *reeko/a*
dentist dentista, el/la *denteesta*
deodorant desodorante, el *desodoranteh*
department store almacén por departamentos, el *almasen por departamentos*
deposit depósito, el *deposeeto*
dessert postre, el *postreh*
to develop (film) revelar *rebelar*
diabetic diabético/a *dyabeteeko/a*
diarrhoea diarrea, la *dyarrea*
diesel gasoil, el *gasoyl*
difficult difícil *deefeeseel*
dining room comedor, el *komedor*
dinner cena, la; (Ecu) merienda, la *sena; meryenda*
direction dirección, la *deereksyon*
disc disco, el *deesko*
dish (food) plato, el *plato*

disinfected desinfectado/a *deseenfektado/a*
to dive bucear *booseear*
divorced divorciado/a *deeborsyado/a*
to do; to make hacer *aser*
doctor doctor/a, el/la *doktor/a*
dollar ($) (US) dólar americano, el *dolar amereekano*
door puerta, la *pwerta*
double doble *dobleh*
dozen docena, la *dosena*
dress vestido, el *besteedo*
to drink beber *beber*
drink bebida, la *bebeeda*
  cold bebida fría, la *bebeeda freea*
  hot bebida caliente, la *bebeeda kalyenteh*
  soft refresco, el; (Arg, Col) gaseosa, la *refresko; gaseosa*
to drive manejar *manehhar*
driver chofer, el/la *tchofer*
driver's licence licencia (de manejar), la; (Arg) registro, el; (Col) pase, el; (Per) brevete, el *leesensya (deh manehhar); rrehheestro; paseh; brebeteh*
to drop caer *kaer*
drops (medical) gotas, las *gotas*
drowsiness somnolencia, la *somnolensya*
dry seco/a *seko/a*
dubbed doblado/a *doblado/a*

E

each, every cada *kada*
ear (inner); ear (outer) oído, el; oreja, la *oeedo; orehha*
earrings aretes, los; (Arg) aros, los *aretes; aros*
earthenware, mud barro, el *barro*
to eat comer *komer*
eggs huevos, los *webos*
embroidered bordado/a *bordado/a*
emergency emergencia, la *emerhhensya*
empty vacío/a *baseeo*
end final, el *feenal*
engine motor, el *motor*
engineer ingeniero/a, el/la *eenhhenyero/a*
England Inglaterra *eenglaterra*
English inglés/esa *eengles/esa*
enjoy your meal! ¡buen provecho! *bwen probetcho*
to enter; to go in entrar *entrar*
entrance entrada, la *entrada*
envelope sobre, el *sobreh*
every (three hours) cada (tres horas) *kada*
every day todos los días *todos los deeas*
everything todo *todo*

to **examine** examinar *eksameenar*
except excepto *esepto*
exchange rate cambio, el *kambyo*
excursion excursión, la *eskoorsyon*
excuse me! ¡perdón! *perdon*
to **exercise** hacer ejercicio *aser ehherseesyo*
exhibition exposición, la *esposeesyon*
expensive caro/a *karola*

F

fair feria, la *ferya*
family familia, la *fameelya*
fan ventilador, el *benteelador*
far lejos *lehhos*
festival festival, el *festeebal*
fill (with) llenar (de) *yenar*
filling (dental) empaste, el; (Arg, Uru) emplomadura, la; (Col) calza, la; (Mex, Chi) tapadura, la *empasteh; emplomadoora; kalsa; tapadoora*
film película, la; (photography) rollo, el *peleekoola; rroyo*
to **finish** terminar *termeenar*
fire! ¡fuego! *fwego*
fireworks fuegos artificiales, los *fwegos arteefeesyales*
first primero/a *preemerola*
first class (coach) de lujo; pullman; de primera clase *deh looho;deh preemera klaseh*
fish pescado, el *peskado*
to **fish** pescar *peskar*
fishing pesca, la *peska*
fishing rod caña de pescar, la *kanya deh peskar*
fitting rooms probadores, los *probadores*
flat (housing) apartamento, el; departamento, el *apartamento; departamento*
flippers aletas, las *aletas*
floor (storey) piso, el *peeso*
flu gripe, la *greepeh*
food comida, la *komeeda*
  baby comida para bebés, la *komeeda para bebes*
food poisoning intoxicación, la *eentokseekasyon*
football fútbol, el *footbol*
football match partido de fútbol, el *parteedo deh footbol*
foreign extranjero/a *estranhherola*
fork tenedor, el *tenedor*
form formulario, el *formoolaryo*
fracture fractura, la *fraktoora*
free (unoccupied) libre; (without payment) gratis *leebreh; gratees*
friend amigo/a *ameegola*
from de *deh*
in front of delante de *delanteh deh*
fruit fruta, la *froota*
full lleno/a *yenola*
fun fair feria de diversiones, la *ferya deh deebersyones*
furniture muebles, los *mwebles*

G

gallery galería, la *galereea*
game juego, el *hhwego*
  video videojuego, el *beedeo-hhwego*
garage taller, el *tayer*
garden jardín, el *hhardeen*
gate puerta, la *pwerta*
Gents caballeros, los; hombres, los *kabayeros; ombres*
to **get off the train/bus** bajarse del tren/autobús *bahharseh del tren/owtoboos*
to **get up** levantarse *lebantarseh*
girl muchacha, la; chica, la *mootchatcha; tcheeka*
glass (water) vaso, el *baso*; (wine) copa, la *kopa*
glasses gafas, las; (Per) lentes, los; (SCon) anteojos, los *gafas; lentes; anteohhos*
sunglasses gafas de sol, las *gafas deh sol*
gloss brillante *breeyanteh*
to **go** ir *eer*
to **go past/through** pasar por *pasar por*
to **go out** salir *saleer*
goggles gafas, las; anteojos de natación, los; (Mex) goggles, los; (SCon) antiparras, las *gafas; anteohhos deh natasyon; gogols; anteeparras*
gold oro, el *oro*
golf golf, el *golf*
golf clubs palos de golf, los *palos deh golf*
good bien *byen*
good afternoon/evening buenas tardes *bwenas tardes*
good evening/night buenas noches *bwenas notches*
good morning buenos días *bwenos deeas*
goodbye adiós *adyos*
gram gramo, el *gramo*
green verde *berdeh*
group grupo, el *groopo*

guide (book) guía, la *geea;* (bus) guía de autobuses, la *geea deh owtobooses;* (person) guía, el/la *geea*

H

hair pelo, el *pelo*

hairdryer secador de pelo, el *sekador deh pelo*

half medio/a; mitad, la *medyola; meetath*

hammock hamaca, la *amaka*

handicrafts artesanías, las *artesaneeas*

handicrafts shop tienda de artesanías, la; (Arg) talabartería, la *tyenda deh artesaneeas; talabartereea*

handmade hecho/a a mano *etchola a mano*

hanger gancho, el; (Arg) percha, la *gantcho; pertcha*

hangover resaca, la; cruda, la; (Col) guayabo, el; (Ven) ratón, el *resaka; krooda; guayabo; rraton*

to have (food) tomar *tomar;* (own) tener *tener*

headache dolor de cabeza, el *dolor deh kabesa*

heart attack infarto, el *eenfarto*

hello! ¡hola! *ola*

to help ayudar *ayoodar*

help! ¡auxilio!; ¡socorro! *owseelyo; sokorro*

hepatitis hepatitis, la *epateetees*

here aquí *akee*

hiking hacer caminatas *aser kameenatas*

to hire alquilar *alkeelar*

HIV positive seropositivo/a *seroposeeteebo*

horse ride cabalgata, la *kabalgata*

horse riding montar a caballo *montar a kabayo*

hostel hostal *ostal*

hot caliente *kalyenteh*
  I'm hot tengo calor *tengo kalor*
  It's hot (weather) hace calor *aseh kalor*
  It's hot (spicy) pica *peeka*

hot dog perro caliente, el; hot dog, el; (Arg) pancho, el *perro kalyenteh; hhot dog; pantcho*

hotel hotel, el *otel*

hour hora, la *ora*

house casa, la *kasa*

to hurt doler *doler*

hurt; injured (a person) herido/a *ereedola*

husband esposo, el *esposo*

I

ice hielo, el *yelo*

ice cream helado, el *elado*

ice-cream cone barquillo, el; (Arg) cucurucho, el *barkeeyo; kookoorootcho*

ice lolly paleta, la *paleta*

if si *see*

to include incluir *eenklooeer*

included incluido/a *eenklooeedola*

infection infección, la *eenfeksyon*

injection inyección, la *eenyeksyon*

insect insecto, el *eensekto*

insect repellent repelente de insectos, el *repelenteh deh eensektos*

insect bite picadura, la *peekadoora*

inside adentro *adentro*

insurance seguro, el *segooro*

to be interested in interesarse en *eenteresarseh en*

internet café café internet, el; cibercafé, el *kafeh eenternet;seeberkafeh*

interval intermedio, el *eentermedyo*

iron plancha, la *plantcha*

island isla, la *eesla*

J

jacket (formal) saco, el *sako*

jacket (casual) chaqueta, la; (Arg) campera, la; (Mex) chamarra, la *tchaketa; kampera; tchamarra*

jam mermelada, la *mermelada*

jar frasco, el *frasko*

jewellery joyas, las *hhoyas*

journey viaje, el *byahheh*

jug jarra, la *hharra*

juice, jugo, el *hhoogo*

jumper suéter, el; (Arg) pulóver, el *sweter; poolober*

K

kayaking piragüismo, el *peeragweesmo*

to keep guardar *gwardar*

keys llaves, las *yabes*

kilo kilo, el *keelo*

kilometre kilómetro, el *keelometro*

kitchen cocina, la *koseena*

knickers pantaletas, las; pantis, los; (Arg) bombacha, la; (Col) calzones, los; (Cub) blúmer, el *pantaletas; pantees; bombatcha; calzones; bloomer*

knife cuchillo, el *kootcheeyo*

to know saber *saber*

L

Ladies damas, las; mujeres, las *damas; moohheres*

lake lago, el *lago*

lamp lámpara, la *lampara*

laptop computadora portátil, la *kompootadora portateel*
to last durar *doorar*
last último/a *oolteemo*
last night anoche *anotcheh*
last week semana pasada, la *semana pasada*
lawyer abogado/a *abogadola*
to leak gotear *gotear*
leather cuero, el; piel, la *kwero; pyel*
to leave (a place) salir de *saleer deh;* (something) dejar *dehhar*
left izquierda, la *eeskyerda*
lemon; lime limón, el *leemon*
letter carta, la *karta*
lift ascensor, el; (Mex) elevador, el *asensor; elebador*
light luz, la *loos;* lights (car) luces, las *looses*
lime limón, el *leemon*
line (underground) línea, la *leenea*
litre litro, el *leetro*
to live vivir *beebeer*
lock (door) cerradura, la *serradoora;* (car door) seguro, el *segooro*
long largo/a *largola*
to look at mirar *meerar*
to lose perder *perder*
lunch almuerzo, el *almwerso*

M

magazine revista, la *rebeesta*
mail correo, el *korreo*
registered correo certificado, el *korreo serteefeekado*
malaria malaria, la; paludismo, el *malarya; paloodeesmo*
man hombre, el *ombreh*
manual (car) mecánico/a *mekaneekola*
map plano, el; mapa, el *plano; mapa*
market mercado, el; (Mex) tianguis, el *merkado; tyangees*
flea mercado de pulgas, el *merkado deh poolgas*
married casado/a *kasadola*
mask máscara, la *maskara;* diving visor, el *beesor*
matches fósforos, los; cerillas, las *fosforos; sereeyas*
matt (photography) mate *mateh*
meal comida, la *komeeda*
mechanic mecánico/a, el/la *mekaneekola*
medication medicamento, el; medicina, la *medeekamento; medeeseena*
medium (clothes) mediano/a *medyanola*

medium (steak) término medio; (Arg) a punto *termeeno medyo; a poonto*
menu carta, la; menú, el *karta; menoo*
children's menú infantil, el *menoo eenfanteel*
of the day menú del día, el *menoo del deea*
midday mediodía *medyo-deea*
in the middle of mediados de, a *medyados deh*
midnight medianoche *medya-notcheh*
milk leche, la *letcheh*
milkshake malteada, la; (Arg) licuado, el *malteada; leekwado*
minigolf golfito, el *golfeeto*
mint tea té de yerbabuena; (Arg) té de menta, el *teh deh yerbabwena; teh deh menta*
Miss señorita *senyoreeta*
mistake error, el *error*
mobile phone celular, el *seloolar*
mobile phone charger cargador de celular, el *kargador deh seloolar*
moisturiser crema humectante, la *krema oomektanteh*
money plata, la; dinero, el *plata; deenero*
monument monumento, el *monoomento*
morning mañana, la *manyana*
motorbike moto, la *moto*
motorway autopista, la; (Arg) ruta, la *owto-peesta; rroota*
mountain montaña, la *montanya*
mountaineering montañismo, el *montanyeesmo*
to move mover *mober*
Mr señor, el *senyor*
Mrs/Ms señora, la *senyora*
mug atracar *atrakar*
mummy momia, la *momya*
museum museo, el *mooseo*
music música, la *mooseeka*
folk música folclórica, la *mooseeka folkloreeka*

N

name nombre, el *nombreh*
napkin servilleta, la *serbeeyeta*
nappy pañal, el *panyal*
nausea náusea, la *nowsea*
near; nearby cercano/a; cerca *serkanola; serka*
to need necesitar *neseseetar*
new nuevo/a *nwebola*
newspaper periódico, el; (Arg) diario, el *peryodeeko; dyaryo*

newspaper stand puesto de periódicos, el *pwesto deh peryodeekos*
next próximo/a *prokseemo/a*
next to junto a; (Arg) al lado de *hhoonto a; al lado deh*
night noche, la *notcheh*
nightclub; club discoteca, la; (Arg) boliche, el *deeskoteka; boleetcheh*
no; not no *no*
nothing nada *nada*
now ahora *aora*
number número, el *noomero*
plate número de placa, el; (Arg) número de patente, el *noomero deh plaka; noomero deh patenteh*
nuts nueces, las *nweses*

O

oil aceite, el *aseyteh*
okay (good) bueno/a *bweno/a*; (appropriate) apto/a *apto/a*
old antiguo/a; viejo/a *anteegwo/a; byehho/a*
only sólo; solamente *solo; solamenteh*
open abierto/a *abyerto/a*
to open abrir *abreer*
operation operación, la *operasyon*
opposite enfrente de *enfrenteh deh*
outside afuera *afwera*
oven horno, el *orno*

P

package; parcel paquete, el *paketeh*
pain dolor, el *dolor*
painkillers calmantes, los; analgésicos, los *kalmantes; analhheseekos*
painting pintura, la *peentoora*
palace palacio, el *palasyo*
papaya papaya, la; (Cub) fruta bomba, la; (Ven) lechosa, la *papaya; froota bomba; letchosa*
paper papel, el *papel*
parade desfile, el *desfeeleh*
paragliding parapente, el *parapenteh*
pardon? ¿cómo? *komo*
park parque, el *parkeh*
to park estacionar; (Col) parquear *estasyonar; parkear*
party fiesta, la *fyesta*
passport pasaporte, el *pasaporteh*
pastry (corn) empanada, la *empanada*
path sendero, el *sendero*
to pay pagar *pagar*
peanuts maní, el; (Mex) cacahuates, los *manee; kakawates*
pedestrian crossing cruce peatonal, el *krooseh peatonal*
pen bolígrafo, el *boleegrafo*

pepper (veg) pimiento, el; (Col) pimentón, el *peemyento; peementon*
pepper (spice) pimienta, la *peemyenta*
person persona, la *persona*
petrol gasolina, la; (Arg) nafta, la; (Chi) bencina, la *gasoleena; nafta; benseena*
unleaded gasolina sin plomo, la *gasoleena seen plomo*
petrol station gasolinera, la; (Arg) estación de servicio, la; (Col) bomba, la; (Per) grifo, el *gasoleenera; estasyon deh serbeesyo; bomba; greefo*
pillow almohada, la *almwada*
pills pastillas, las *pasteeyas*
pineapple piña, la; (Arg) ananá, el (f) *peenya; anana*
pink rosa *rrosa*
pistachio pistacho, el *peestatcho*
place lugar, el *loogar*
plasters curitas, las *kooreetas*
plate plato, el *plato*
platform andén, el; (Arg) plataforma, la *anden; plataforma*
to play jugar *hhoogar*
please por favor *por fabor*
police station comisaría de policía, la; (Mex) delegación de policía, la *komeesareea deh poleeseea; delegasyon deh poleeseea*
poncho poncho, el; (Col) ruana, la; (Mex) sarape, el *pontcho; rwana; sarapeh*
port puerto, el *pwerto*
post box buzón, el *booson*
post office correo, el *korreo*
postage stamp estampilla, la *estampeeya*
pottery; earthenware cerámica, la; barro, el *serameeka; barro*
pound (£) libra, la *leebra*
to prefer preferir *prefereer*
pregnant embarazada *embarasada*
to prescribe recetar *rresetar*
price precio, el *presyo*
to print imprimir *eempreemeer*
procession procesión, la *prosesyon*
programme programa, el *programa*
to puncture ponchar; (Arg) pinchar *pontchar; peentchar*
purified purificado/a *pooreefeekado/a*
purse monedero, el *monedero*
to put poner *poner*
pyramids pirámides, las *peerameedes*

Q

quickly! ¡rápido! *rrapeedo*
quite, rather bastante *bastanteh*

R

race (horse/car) carrera, la *karrera*
racket raqueta, la *rraketa*
rare (steak) poco hecho/a; (Arg) jugoso/a *poko etchola; hhoogosola*
rash salpullido, el *salpooyeedo*
raw crudo/a *kroodola*
razors afeitadoras, las; cuchillas, las *afaytadoras; kootcheeyas*
  disposable cuchillas desechables, las *kootcheeyas desetchables*
ready listo/a *leestola*
really? ¿de verdad? *deh berdath*
receipt recibo, el *rreseebo*
to recommend recomendar *rrekomendar*
red rojo/a *rrohhola*
reduction; discount descuento, el *deskwento*
remedy; medicine remedio, el *rremedyo*
to rent rentar *rrentar*
to repair arreglar *arreglar*
to repeat repetir *rrepeteer*
reservation; booking reservación, la; (Arg) reserva, la *rreserbasyon; rreserba*
to rest descansar *deskansar*
restaurant restaurante, el *restowranteh*
to return; come back volver *bolber*
right derecha, la *deretcha*
river río, el *rreeo*
road carretera, la; (Arg) ruta, la *karretera; rroota*
robbery robo, el *rrobo*
rock climbing escalada de roca, la *eskalada deh rroka*
room habitación, la; (inf) cuarto, el *abeetasyon; kwarto*
  single habitación individual, la *abeetasyon eendeebeedwal*
  double habitación doble, la *abeetasyon doble*
room service servicio a la habitación, el *serbeesyo a la abeetasyon*
rope cuerda, la *kwerda*
roundabout glorieta, la; rotonda, la *gloryeta; rrotonda*
row, line fila, la *feela*
rucksack mochila, la *motcheela*
rug tapete, el; alfombra, la *tapeteh; alfombra*
ruins ruinas, las *rweenas*

S

safe-deposit box caja fuerte, la; caja de seguridad, la *kahha fwerteh; kahha deh segooreedath*
sailing navegación en vela, la *nabegasyon en bela*
salad ensalada, la *ensalada*
salt sal, la *sal*
sandals sandalias, las; (Mex) huaraches, los *sandalyas; waratches*
sandwich; roll sándwich, el; (Mex) tortas, las *sandweetch; tortas*
scooter moto scooter, la *moto eskooter*
scorpion alacrán, el *alakran*
sea mar, el *mar*
seafood comida de mar, la *komeeda deh mar*
seat asiento, el; puesto, el *asyento; pwesto*
to see ver *ber*
to sell vender *bender*
to send mandar *mandar*
senior citizens pensionados, los *pensyonados*
separate; extra aparte; adicional *aparteh; adeesyonal*
serious grave *grabeh*
service; service charge servicio, el *serbeesyo*
set (pictures) copias, las *kopyas*
shampoo champú, el *tchampoo*
shawl chal, el; (Mex) rebozo, el *tchal; reboso*
shivers escalofríos, los *eskalofreeos*
to shop ir de compras *eer deh kompras*
shop tienda, la; (Arg) comercio, el *tyenda; komersyo*
shopping centre centro comercial, el *sentro komersyal*
short (length) corto/a *kortola*
show espectáculo, el *espektakoolo*
shower ducha, la; (Mex) regadera, la *dootcha; rregadera*
to be sick vomitar *bomeetar*
sickness enfermedad, la *enfermedath*
  travel mareo, el *mareo*
side effects efectos secundarios, los; contraindicaciones, las *efektos sekoondaryos; kontra-eendeekasyones*
to sign firmar *feermar*
silk seda, la *seda*
silver plata, la *plata*
single soltero/a *solterola*
sink; washbasin lavamanos, el *labamanos*

size (clothes) talla, la *taya;* (shoes) número, el *noomero*

to ski; skiing esquiar *eskyar*

ski boots botas de esquí, las *botas deh eskee*

ski resort estación de esquí, la *estasyon deh eskee*

skis esquís, los *eskees*

skirt falda, la; (Arg) pollera, la *falda; poyera*

to sleep dormir *dormeer*

slowly despacio *despasyo*

small pequeño/a; chico/a *pekenyola; tcheekola*

to smoke fumar *foomar*

smoking/no smoking fumar/no fumar *foomar/no foomar*

snorkel esnórkel, el *esnorkel*

snorkelling bucear con esnórkel *boosear kon esnorkel*

soap jabón, el *hhabon*

sold out agotado/a *agotadola*

someone; somebody alguien *algyen*

something; rather algo *algo*

son hijo, el *eehho*

sorbet granizado, el; sorbete, el; (Mex, Cub, PtR) nieve, la *graneesado; sorbete; nyebeh*

sorry perdone *perdoneh*

spa balneario, el *balnearyo*

Spanish español/a; (language, Arg) castellano, el *espanyolla; kasteyano*

spare parts repuestos, los; refacciones, las *rrepwestos; rrefaksyones*

speed velocidad, la *beloseedath*

to be spicy picar *peekar*

spoon cuchara, la *kootchara*

sprain (ankle) esguince, el *esgeenseh*

square plaza, la *plasa*
   main plaza mayor, la; (Arg/Per) plaza de armas, la; (Mex) zócalo, el *plasa mayor; plasa deh armas; sokalo*

staircase escalera, la *eskalera*

to start (car) arrancar *arrankar*

to start; to begin empezar *empesar*

station (train) estación, la *estasyon*

to stay quedarse *kedarseh*

to steal; to rob robar *rrobar*

steering wheel timón, el; (Mex and SCon) volante, el *teemon; bolanteh*

to sting picar *peekar*

stop alto; pare *alto; pareh*

stop (bus/train) parada, la *parada*

straight away ya mismo; enseguida; ahorita *ya meesmo; ensegeeda; aoreeta*

straw paja, la *pahha*

strawberry fresa, la; (SCon) frutilla, la *fresa; frooteeya*

street calle, la *kayeh*

student estudiante, el/la *estoodyanteh*

subtitles subtítulos, los *soobteetoolos*

sugar azúcar, el (f) *asookar*

suit traje, el *trahhe*

to suit (clothes/colours) quedar *kedar*

to suit, to go with quedar bien *kedar byen*

suitcase maleta la; (Arg) valija, la *maleta; baleehha*

summer verano, el *berano*

sun sol, el *sol*

sun cream crema anti solar, la *krema antee-solar*

sun block bloqueador solar, el *blokeador solar*

sun lounger reposera, la; silla de playa, la *reposera; seeya deh playa*

suntan lotion bronceador, el *bronseador*

sunburn quemaduras del sol, las *kemadooras del sol*

sunshade sombrilla, la; parasol, el *sombreeya; parasol*

sunstroke insolación, la *eensolasyon*

supermarket supermercado, el *soopermerkado*

supplement cargo adicional, el; recargo, el *kargo adeesyonal; rrekargo*

surfing hacer surfing *aser sorfeen*

to swallow tragar *tragar*

sweet dulce, el *doolseh*

to swim; swimming nadar *nadar*

swimming costume traje de baño, el; (Arg) malla (de natación), la; (Col) vestido de baño, el; (Cub) trusa, la *trahhe deh banyo; maya (deh natasyon); besteedo deh banyo; troosa*

swimming pool piscina, la; (Arg) pileta, la; (Mex) alberca, la *peeseena; peeleta; alberka*

symptoms síntomas, los *seentomas*

syrup; medicine jarabe, el *hharabeh*

T

table mesa, la *mesa*

tablecloth mantel, el *mantel*

tablet pastilla, la *pasteeya*

to take (grab) tomar *tomar*

to talk; to speak hablar *ablar*

tampons tampones, los *tampones*

tap llave (del agua), la; (Arg) canilla, la *yabeh (del agwa); kaneeya*

taxes impuestos, los *eempwestos*

taxi taxi, el *taksee*

taxi rank sitio de taxis, el *seetyo deh taksees*

teacher profesor/a, el/la *profesorla*

teaspoon cucharita, la *kootchareeta*

teaspoonful cucharadita, la *kootcharadeeta*

telephone teléfono, el *telefono*

to telephone; to call llamar *yamar*

television televisión, la *telebeesyon*

temperature; fever fiebre, la; calentura, la *fyebreh; kalentoora*

tennis tenis, el *tenees*

tennis court cancha de tenis, la *kantcha deh tenees*

tent tienda (de campaña), la; (Arg, Col) carpa, la *tyenda (deh kampanya); karpa*

tetanus tétano, el *tetano*

textiles telas, las *telas*

thank you gracias *grasyas*

theatre teatro, el *teatro*

theft robo, el *rrobo*

thermal baths aguas termales, las *agwas termales*

thief ladrón, el *ladron*

to think pensar *pensar*

this este/a *esteh/a*

this morning esta mañana *esta manyana*

ticket (concert/film/coach) entrada, la; boleto, el *entrada; boleto;* (plane) billete, el; pasaje, el *beeyeteh; pasahheh*

single/return boleto de ida/de ida y vuelta, el *boleto deh eeda/ deh eeda ee bwelta*

ticket office taquilla, la; (Arg) ventanilla, la *takeeya; bentaneeya*

time tiempo, el *tyempo*

times (three times) veces, las (tres veces) *beses (tres beses)*

timetable horario, el *oraryo*

tin lata, la *lata*

today hoy *oy*

toffee caramelo, el *karamelo*

toilet inodoro, el; (Mex) excusado, el *eenodoro; eskoosado*

toilet paper papel higiénico, el *papel eehhyeeneeko*

toilet; bathroom baño, el *banyo*

toll (road) peaje, el; (Mex) cuota, la *peahheh; kwota*

toll booth caseta (de cobro), la; (Arg) cabina (de cobro de peaje), la *kaseta (deh kobro); kabeena (de kobro deh peahheh)*

tomato tomate, el; (Mex) jitomate, el *tomateh; hheetomateh*

tomorrow mañana *manyana*

tonight esta noche *esta notcheh*

too; as well también *tambyen*

toothpaste pasta dental, la; dentífrico, el *pasta dental; denteefreeko*

toothbrush cepillo de dientes, el *sepeeyo deh dyentes*

tour tour, el *toor*

tourist information office oficina de turismo, la *ofeeseena deh tooreesmo*

towel toalla, la *toaya*

sanitary toallas higiénicas/ sanitarias, las *toayas eehhyeneekas/ saneetaryas*

tower torre, la *torreh*

town centre centro, el *sentro*

town hall municipalidad, la; alcaldía, la; (Carib) ayuntamiento, el; (Mex) presidencia municipal, la *mooneeseepaleedath; alkaldeea; ayoontamyento; preseedensya mooneeseepal*

track sendero, el; (Col) brecha, la *sendero; bretcha*

traditional típico/a *teepeeko/a*

traffic light semáforo, el *semaforo*

train tren, el *tren*

to travel viajar *byahhar*

travellers' cheques cheques de viaje, los *tchekes deh byahheh*

trip viaje, el *byahheh*

truth verdad, la *berdath*

to try on probarse *probarseh*

T-shirt camiseta, la; playera, la; (Arg) remera, la *kameeseta; playera; remera*

to turn something on encender; prender *ensender; prender*

twice dos veces *dos beses*

type tipo, el *teepo*

typhoid tifoidea, la *teefoydea*

tyre llanta, la; (Arg) rueda, la *yanta; rweda*

U

underground metro, el; (Arg) subte, el *metro; soobteh*

V

vaccinated against vacunado/a contra *bakoonado/a kontra*

vanilla vainilla, la *biyneeya*

vase jarrón, el *hharron*

VAT IVA, el *eeba*

vegan végano/a *begano/a*

vegetarian vegetariano/a *behhetaryano/a*

very muy *mwee*

viewpoint mirador, el *meerador*

villa villa, la *beeya*

to visit visitar *beeseetar*

visit visita, la *beseeta*

W

waiter/waitress mesero/a, el/la; (Arg) mozo/a, el/la *mesero/a; moso/a*

wallet cartera, la; billetera, la *kartera; beeyetera*

washing powder detergente de ropa, el; jabón para la ropa, el *deterhhenteh deh rropa; hhabon para la rropa*

washing-up liquid líquido lavaplatos, el; (Arg) detergente, el *leekeedo laba-platos; deterhhenteh*

watch reloj, el *rrelohh*

watch out! ¡cuidado! *kweedado*

water agua, el (f) *agwa*

waterfall cascada, la *kaskada*

waterskiing esquí acuático, el *eskee akwateeko*

water-skis esquís acuáticos, los *eskees akwateekos*

week semana, la *semana*

weekend fin de semana, el *feen deh semana*

welcome bienvenido/a *byen-beneedo/a*

well done (steak) bien hecho/a; (Arg) cocido/a *byen etcho; koseedo/a*

wheat trigo, el *treego*

wheelchair silla de ruedas, la *seeya deh rwedas*

when? ¿cuándo? *kwando*

white blanco/a *blanko/a*

whole entero/a *entero/a*

Wi Fi modem inalámbrico, el; internet inalámbrico, el *modem eenalambreeko; eenternet eenalambreeko*

wife esposa, la *esposa*

window ventana, la *bentana*

windsurf board tabla de wind-surf, la *tabla deh ween sorf*

winter invierno, el *eenbyerno*

with con *kon*

without sin *seen*

woman; wife mujer, la *moohher*

wood madera, la *madera*

wool lana, la *lana*

work trabajo, el *trabahho*

to work (function) funcionar *foonsyonar*

workshop taller, el *tayer*

to write escribir *eskreebeer*

Y

year año, el *anyo*

yellow amarillo/a *amareeyo/a*

yellow fever fiebre amarilla, la *fyebreh amareeya*

yes sí *see*

yesterday ayer *ayer*

youth hostel villa juvenil, la; albergue, el *beeya hhoobeneel; albergeh*

A

a to
abierto/a open
abogado/a lawyer
abrir to open
accidente, el accident
aceite, el oil
aceptar to accept
acondicionador, el conditioner
adaptador de corriente, el current
  adaptor
adentro inside
adicional separate; extra
adiós goodbye
adulto, el adult
aeropuerto, el airport
afeitadoras, las disposable razors
afuera outside
agotado/a sold out
agua, el (f) water
aguas termales, las thermal baths
ahora now
ahorita straight away
aire acondicionado, el air conditioned
ají, el chilli
al lado de next to
alacrán, el scorpion
alberca, la swimming pool (Mex)
albergue, el B&B; youth hostel
alcaldía, la town hall
alérgico/a allergic
aletas, las flippers
alfombra, la rug
algo something; rather
algodón, el cotton
alguien someone; somebody
almohada, la pillow
almuerzo, el lunch
alquilar to hire
¡alto! stop!
amarillo/a yellow
ambulancia, la ambulance
amigo/a friend
analgésico, el painkiller
ananá, el pineapple (Arg)
andén, el platform
anteojos, los glasses (SCon)
anteojos de natación, los goggles
antes before
antibióticos, los antibiotics
antiguo/a old; ancient
antihistamínico, el antihistamine
antiparras, las goggles (SCon)
año, el year
apartamento, el flat (housing)
aparte separate; extra
apto/a okay (appropriate)

aquí here
aros, los earrings (Arg)
arrancar to start (car)
arreglar to repair
arte, el art
artesanías, las handicrafts
asaltar to attack
ascensor, el lift
asiento, el seat
asma, el asthma
aspirina, la aspirin
atracar to mug
auto, el car (SCon)
autobús, el bus
automático/a automatic
autopista, la motorway
¡auxilio! help!
avión, el aeroplane
ayudar to help
ayuntamiento, el town hall (Carib)
azúcar, el sugar
azul blue

B

bajarse to get off (train/bus)
bajo/a low
balneario, el spa
bálsamo, el conditioner
banco, el bank
baño, el toilet; bathroom
bar, el bar
barato/a cheap
barco, el boat
barquillo, el (ice-cream) cone
barro, el pottery; earthenware
bastante quite; rather
basurero, el dustbin; rubbish bin
batería, la battery (car)
beber to drink
bebida, la drink
  caliente/fría hot/cold
beige beige
bencina, la petrol (Chi)
bicicleta, la bicycle
bicicleta de montaña, la mountain
  bike
bien good
bien hecho/a well done (steak)
bienvenido/a welcome
billete, el ticket (for travelling)
binoculares, los binoculars
bistec, el beefsteak
blanco/a white
bloqueador solar, el sun cream/block
blúmer, el knickers (Cub)
boleto, el ticket
  de ida/de ida y vuelta single/return
boliche, el nightclub (Arg)

bolígrafo, el pen
bolsa, la bag; shoulder bag; handbag
  de dormir sleeping bag
bolso, el shoulder bag
bomba (de gasolina), la petrol station
  (Col)
bombacha, la knickers (Arg)
bordado/a embroidered
botas, las boots
  de esquí ski boots
botella, la bottle
brecha, la track (Col)
brevete, el driver's licence (Per)
brillante gloss
bronceador, el suntan lotion
bucear to dive
  con esnórkel snorkelling
¡buen provecho! enjoy your meal!
bueno/a okay
buenos días/buenas tardes/buenas
  noches good morning/good afternoon;
  evening/good evening; night
bufé, el buffet
buzón, el post box

C
cabalgata, la horse ride
caballeros, los Gents
cabeza, la head
cabina (de cobro de peaje), la toll booth
  (Arg)
cacahuates, los peanuts (Mex)
cada each, every
caer en pana to break down (Chi)
caerse to drop; to fall
café brown
café, el café (restaurant)
café internet, el internet café
cafetería, la coffee shop
caja de seguridad, la; caja fuerte, la
  safe-deposit box
cajero automático, el cash-point
calentura, la temperature, fever
caliente hot
calmantes, los painkillers
calza, la filling (dental) (Col)
calzones, los underpants; knickers
  (Col)
calle, la street
cama, la bed
  doble/matrimonial double
  individual single
cámara, la camera
  digital digital
  desechable disposable
cambiar to change
cambio, el exchange rate
cambúr, el banana (Ven)

camión, el bus (Mex)
campera, la jacket (Arg)
camping, el campsite
canasta, la basket
cancha de tenis, la tennis court
canilla, la tap (Arg)
cantina, la bar (Mex)
caña de pescar, la fishing rod
caramelo, el toffee
cargador de celular, el charger (mobile)
cargo adicional, el supplement
carnaval, el carnival
carnet (de estudiante), el student card
caro/a expensive
carpa, la tent (Arg, Col)
carrera, la race
carretera, la road
carro, el car (CAm, And)
carta, la letter; menu
cartera, la wallet; handbag
casa, la house
  de huéspedes guest house
  particular guest house (Cub)
casa de cambio, la bureau de change
casado/a married
cascada, la waterfall
caseta (de cobro), la toll booth
castellano, el Spanish language (Arg)
castillo, el castle
catedral, la cathedral
cena, la dinner
centro comercial, el shopping centre
centro, el town centre
cepillo de dientes, el toothbrush
cerámica, la ceramics
cerca; cercano/a close; nearby
cerillas, las matches
cerrado/a closed
cerradura, la lock (door)
cerrar to close
cibercafé, el internet café
ciclismo de montaña, el mountain
  biking
cine, el cinema
cita, la appointment
ciudad, la city
¡claro! of course!
cobija, la blanket
cobre, el copper
coche, el car (Mex, Carib)
cocido/a well done (steak) (Arg)
cocina, la kitchen; cooker
colectivo, el bus (Arg)
comedor, el dining room
comer to eat
comercio, el shop (Arg)
comida, la food; meal
  de mar seafood

comisaría de policía, la police station
¿cómo? pardon?
¿cómo está? how are you?
comprar to buy
computadora portátil, la laptop
con with
concierto, el concert
condón, el condom
contener to contain
contraindicaciones, las side-effects
copias, las set (pictures)
corpiño, el bra (Arg)
correo, el mail
  certificado registered
corridas de toros, las bullfighting
cortarse to cut oneself
corto/a short (length)
costa, la coast
creer to believe
crema, la cream (food); cream
  (medical); ointment
crema
  anti solar sun
  de afeitar shaving
  post solar; para después del sol
  aftersun
creo I think
cruce de caminos, el crossroads
cruce peatonal, el pedestrian crossing
cruda, la hangover
crudo/a raw
cruzar to cross
¿cuándo? when?
¿cuánto? how much?
¿cuánto cuesta(n)? how much does
  it/they cost?
cuarto, el room (informal)
cucharadita, la teaspoonful
cuchillas desechables, las disposable
  razors
cucurucho, el (ice-cream) cone (Arg)
cuenta, la bill
cuerda, la rope
cuero, el leather
cuerpo, el body
¡cuidado! watch out!
cuna, la cot
cuota, la toll (road) (Mex)
curitas, las plasters
chal, el shawl
chamarra, la jacket (Mex)
champú, el shampoo
chaqueta (de cuero), la (leather)
  jacket
chico/a small
chico/a, el/la boy/girl
chile, el chilli
chocolate, el chocolate; hot chocolate

chófer, el/la driver
choqué I crashed

D

damas, las Ladies
dañado/a damaged
dañarse to break down
de from
de lujo first class (coach)
de nada you're welcome
¿de verdad? really?
debe you should
dejar to leave
delante de in front of
delegación de policía, la police station
  (Mex)
dentífrico, el toothpaste
dentista, el/la dentist
departamento, el flat (housing)
depósito, el deposit
derecha, la right
desayuno, el breakfast
descansar to rest
descenso en rapel, el abseiling
descomponerse to break down (Mex)
descuento, el reduction; discount
desfile, el parade
deshidratado/a dehydrated
desinfectado/a disinfected
desodorante, el deodorant
despacio slowly
después after
desviación, la detour
desvío, el detour
detergente de ropa, el washing
  powder
detergente, el washing-up liquid
  (Arg)
detrás de behind
día, el day
diabético/a diabetic
diario, el newspaper (Arg)
diarrea, la diarrhoea
dientes, los teeth
difícil difficult
dirección, la direction; address
disco, el cd; disc
discoteca, la nightclub
divorciado/a divorced
doblado/a dubbed
doble double
docena, la dozen
doctor/a, el/la doctor
dólar americano, el US dollar
doler to hurt
dolor, el ache; pain
dolor de cabeza, el headache
¿dónde (está). . .? where (is) . . . ?

dormir to sleep
dos veces twice
droguería, la chemist's
ducha, la shower
duele it hurts
dulce, el sweet
dura ... it lasts ...
durar to last

E

efectos secundarios, los side effects
elevador, el lift
embarazada pregnant
embotellado/a bottled (drink)
emergencia, la emergency
empanada, la corn pastry
empaste, el filling (dental)
empezar to start; to begin
empieza it starts
emplomadura, la filling (dental) (Arg, Uru)
encaje lace
encender to turn something on
endulzante, el artificial sweetener
enfrente de opposite
enseguida straight away
entero/a whole
entrada, la ticket (concert/film/event); entrance
entrar to come in; to enter; to go in
error, el mistake
escalada de roca, la rock climbing
escalera, la staircase
escalofríos, los shivers
escribir to write
esguince, el sprain (ankle)
esnórkel, el snorkel
espalda, la back (medical)
español/a Spanish
espectáculo, el show
esposo/a, el/la husband/wife
esquí acuático, el waterskiing
esquiar to ski; skiing
esquina, la corner
esquís, los skis
   acuáticos water-skis
esta mañana this morning
estación, la station (train)
estación de esquí, la ski resort
estación de servicio, la petrol station (Arg)
estacionamiento, el car park
estacionar to park
estampilla, la postage stamp
estancia, la B&B ranch (SCon)
estar to be
estómago, el stomach
estrellé I crashed
estreñido/a constipated

estudiante, el/la student
estufa, la cooker
examinar to examine
excepto except
excursión, la excursion
excusado, el toilet (Mex)
exposición, la exhibition
extranjero/a foreign

F

faltar to be lacking
familia, la family
farmacia, la chemist's
feria, la fair
   de diversiones funfair
festival, el festival
fiebre, la temperature, fever
fiebre amarilla, la yellow fever
fiesta, la fiesta; party
fila, la row; line; queue
fin de semana, el weekend
final, el end
a fines de at the end of
firma, la signature
firmar to sign
formulario, el form
fósforos, los matches
fractura, la fracture
frasco, el jar
frazada, la blanket (Arg)
frenar to brake
frenos, los brakes
frío/a cold
fruta bomba, la papaya (Cub)
frutilla, la strawberry (SCon)
¡fuego! fire!
fuegos artificiales, los fireworks
fumar to smoke
   fumar/no fumar smoking/no smoking
funcionar to work (function)
fútbol, el football

G

gafas, las glasses
   de natación goggles
   de sol sunglasses
galería, la gallery
   de arte art
gancho, el hanger
gaseosa, la soft drink (Arg, Col)
gasoil, el diesel
gasolina (sin plomo), la (unleaded) petrol
gasolinera, la petrol station
glorieta, la roundabout
goggles, los goggles (Mex)
golf, el golf
golfito, el mini-golf
gotas, las drops (medical)

gotear to leak
gracias thank you
gramo, el gram
grande big; large
granizado, el sorbet
gratis free (without payment)
grave serious
grifo, el petrol station (Per)
gripe, la flu
grupo, el group
guagua, la bus (Carib)
guardar to leave; to keep
guardarropa, el cloakroom
guayabo, el hangover (Col)
guía, el/la guide (person)
guía, la guide (book)
de autobuses bus
guineo, el banana (Carib)

H

habitación, la room
doble double
individual single
hablar to talk; to speak
hace (calor/frío) it's (hot/cold)
hace (dos horas) (two hours) ago
hacer to do; to make
caminatas to hike
ejercicio to exercise
hacienda, la farm
hamaca, la hammock
hamburguesa, la burger
hasta luego see you later
hasta mañana see you tomorrow
¿hay ...? is there/are there ...?
hay que ... it is necessary to ...
hecho/a a mano handmade
helado, el ice cream
hepatitis, la hepatitis
herido/a hurt; injured
hielo, el ice
hijo/a, el/la son/daughter
hojalata, la tin-plate
¡hola! hello!
hombre, el man
hora, la hour
horario, el timetable
horno, el oven
hospedaje (familiar), el inn
hospedería, la guest house
hostal, el hostel
hostería, la guest house
huaraches, los sandals (peasant
type) (Mex)
hueso, el bone

I

iglesia, la church
imprimir to print

impuestos, los taxes
incluido/a included
incluir to include
incluye it includes
infarto, el heart attack
infección, la infection
ingeniero/a, el/la engineer
inodoro, el toilet
insolación, la sunstroke
interesarse en to be interested in
intermedio, el interval
internet inalámbrico, el Wi Fi
intersección de vías, la crossroads
intoxicación, la food poisoning
invierno, el winter
inyección, la injection
ir to go
de compras to go shopping
isla, la island
IVA, el VAT
izquierda, la left

J

jabón, el soap
jabón para la ropa, el washing
powder
jamón, el ham
jarabe, el syrup
para la tos cough mixture
jardín, el garden
jarrón, el vase
jitomate, el tomato (Mex)
juego, el game
jugar to play
jugo, el juice,
jugo, el juice
jugoso/a rare (steak) (Arg)
junto a next to

K

kilo, el kilo
kilómetro, el kilometre

L

lácteos, los dairy
ladrón, el thief
lago, el lake
lámpara, la lamp
lana, la wool
lancha, la small boat
de motor motor boat
larga distancia, la long distance
lata, la tin
latón, el brass
lavamanos, el sink; washbasin
laxante, el laxative
le falta you/it need(s)
leche, la milk
lechosa, la papaya (Ven)

lejos far
lentes, los glasses (Per)
levantarse to get up
libra, la British pound (£)
libre free (unoccupied)
libro, el book
licencia (de manejar), la driver's license
licuado, el smoothie; milk shake (Arg)
llamar to telephone/call
llamarse to be called
llámeme call me
llanta, la tyre
llave (del agua), la tap
llegar to arrive
llenar (de) to fill (with)
lleno/a full
lleva (pollo) it's got (chicken) in it
llevar to carry, to take
limpiar to clean
línea, la line (underground)
líquido lavaplatos, el washing-up liquid
líquido para lentes de contacto, el
  contact lens solution
listo/a ready
litro, el litre
luces, las lights (car)
lugar, el place
luz, la light

M

madera, la wood
malaria, la malaria
maleta la suitcase
malo/a bad
malla (de natación), la swimming
  costume (Arg)
mandar to send
manejar to drive
maní, el peanut(s)
mano derecha, a on the right
mano izquierda, a on the left
manteca, la butter (Arg)
mantel, el tablecloth
mantequilla, la butter
mañana, la morning
mapa, el map
mar, el sea
mareo, el travel sickness
marrón brown
máscara, la mask
mate matt (photography)
mecánico/a manual (car)
mecánico/a, el/la mechanic (person)
media botella, la half a bottle
media docena, la half a dozen
a mediados de in the middle of
mediano/a medium (clothes)
medianoche, la midnight

medicamento, el medication
medicina, la medicine
medio/a half
medio kilo, el half a kilo
mediodía, el midday
menú menu
  del día of the day
  infantil children's
  turístico! tourist
mercado (de pulgas), el (flea) market
merienda, la dinner (Ecu)
mermelada, la jam
mesa, la table
mesero/a, el/la waiter/waitress
metro, el underground
miel, la honey
mirador, el viewpoint
mirar to look at
mitad, la half
mochila, la rucksack
modem inalámbrico, el Wi Fi
momia, la mummy
moneda, la coin
montaña, la mountain
montañismo, el mountaineering
montar a caballo horse riding
monumento, el monument
morder to bite
moto, la motorbike
moto scooter, la scooter
motor, el engine
mover to move
mozo/a, el/la waiter/waitress (Arg)
muchacho/a, el/la boy/girl
mucho/a a lot
mucho gusto pleased to meet you
mueble, el piece of furniture
mujer, la woman; wife
municipalidad, la town hall
museo, el museum
música (folclórica), la (folk) music
muy very

N

nada nothing
nafta, la petrol (Arg)
náusea, la nausea
navegación en vela, la sailing
Navidad, la Christmas
necesitar (necesito/necesita) to need
  (I need/you need)
negro/a black
nieve, la sorbet (Mex, Cub, PtR)
niño/a, el/la child
no no; not
no funciona it doesn't work
no hay paso no entry
no importa it doesn't matter

no sé I don't know
no se preocupe don't worry
noche, la night
nombre, el name
nos vemos (mañana) see you
  (tomorrow)
nueces, las nuts
nuevo/a new
número, el number; size (shoes)
número de patente, el number plate
  (Arg)
número de placa, el number plate

O

oficina de turismo, la tourist
  information office
¡oiga! hey!
operación, la operation
oro, el gold

P

pagar to pay
paja, la straw
palacio, el palace
paleta, la ice lolly
palos de golf, los golf clubs
palta, la avocado (SCon, Bolivia)
paludismo, el malaria
pancho, el hot dog (Arg)
pañal, el nappy
papas fritas, las chips; crisps
papel, el paper
  higiénico toilet
paquete, el parcel; packet; package
para en it stops at
para llevar to take away
para servirle you're welcome
parada, la (bus/train) stop
parapente, el paragliding
parasol, el sunshade
¡pare! stop!
parque, el park
parquear to park (Col)
partido de fútbol, el football match
pasado mañana the day after
  tomorrow
pasaje, el ticket (for travelling)
pasaporte, el passport
pasar por to go past/through
pase, el driver's licence (Col)
pase por aquí come this way
paseo, el stroll, walk
pasta dental, la toothpaste
pastillas, las pills
peaje, el toll (road)
película, la film
¡peligro! danger!
peligroso/a dangerous
pelo, el hair

pelota, la ball (sports)
pensar to think
pensarlo to think about it
pensión, la boarding house
pensionado/a, el/la senior citizen
pequeño/a small
percha, la hanger (Arg)
perder to lose
Perdí … I've lost …
¡perdón!; ¡perdone! sorry! excuse
  me!
periódico, el newspaper
pero but
perro, el dog
  caliente hot dog
persiana, la blind
persona, la person
pesca, la fishing
pescado, el fish
pescar to fish; go fishing
picadura, la insect bite
picante, el chilli
picar to be spicy/hot
picar to sting
piel, la leather; skin
pila, la battery
pileta, la swimming pool (Arg)
pimentón, el pepper (veg) (Col)
pinchar to puncture (Arg)
pintado/a painted
pintura, la painting
piragüismo, el kayaking
pirámides, las pyramids
piscina, la swimming pool
piso, el floor (storey)
plancha, la iron
plano, el plan; map
planta baja, la ground floor
plata, la silver; money
plataforma, la platform (Arg)
plato dish
  principal main course
playa, la beach
playera, la T-shirt
plaza, la square
plaza de armas, la main square (Per,
  Arg)
plaza mayor, la main square
pocillo, el cup (Col, Per)
poco, un a little
poco hecho/a rare (steak)
pollera, la skirt (Arg)
pomada, la cream (medical);
  ointment
ponchar to puncture; burst (a tyre)
poncho, el poncho
poner to put (on)
ponerse to put on (oneself)

por favor please
porción, la portion
portafolio, el briefcase
posada, la rural house/lodge
precio, el price
preferir to prefer
prender to turn something on
preservativo, el condom
presidencia municipal, la town hall (Mex)
primer piso, el ground floor
primera clase first class (coach/train)
a principios de at the beginning of
probadores, los fitting rooms
probarse to try on (clothes)
procesión, la procession
profesor/a, el/la teacher
programa, el programme
prohibido estacionar no parking
próximo/a next
¿puede . . .? can/could you . . . ?
puedo I can
puente, el bridge
puerta, la door; gate
puerto, el port
puesto, el seat; stall
pullman first class (coach)
pulóver, el jumper (Arg)
punto, a medium (steak) (Arg)
purificado/a purified

Q
¿qué? what?
quedar to suit (clothes, colours)
quedar bien to suit, go with
quedarse to stay
quemaduras del sol, las sunburn
quemarse to burn oneself
queso, el cheese
quiero I want; I'd like
quisiera I'd like

R
rabia, la rabies
radiador, el radiator (car)
¡rápido! quickly!
raqueta, la racket
ratón, el hangover (Ven)
rebozo, el shawl (Mex)
recargo, el supplement
recepcionista, el/la receptionist
recetar to prescribe
recibo, el receipt
recomendar to recommend
refacciones, las spare parts
refresco, el soft drink
regadera, la shower (Mex)
registro, el driver's licence (Arg)
remedio, el remedy, medicine

remera, la T-shirt (Arg)
rentar to rent
repelente de insectos, el insect repellent
repetir to repeat
reposera, la sun lounger
repuestos, los spare parts
resaca, la hangover
reserva, la reservation; booking
reservación, la reservation; booking
resfriado, el cold (medical)
respirar to breath
restaurante, el restaurant
retorcijones, los stomach cramps
revelar to develop (film)
revisar to check
revista, la magazine
rico/a delicious
riñón, el kidney
río, el river
robar to steal; to rob
robo, el robbery; theft
rojo/a red
rollo, el (camera) film
romper to break
romperse to break down (Arg)
rosa pink
roto/a broken
rotonda, la roundabout
ruana, la poncho (Col)
rueda, la tyre (Arg)
ruinas, las ruins
ruta, la road; motorway (Arg)

S
saber to know
sabor, el flavour
sacar to take out
sacarina, la artificial sweetener
sal, la salt
salir to leave, to go out
salón de baile, el dance hall
salpullido, el rash
¡salud! cheers!
sandalias, las sandals
sándwich, el sandwich; roll
sarape, el poncho (Mex)
secador de pelo, el hairdryer
seco/a dry
seda, la silk
segundo/a second
seguro, el insurance
seguros, los locks (car doors)
semáforo, el traffic light
semana, la week
  pasada) last
  que viene), la next
sendero, el path; track

al de desvío, la detour sign
ior, el Mr
ora, la Mrs; Ms
orita, la Miss
  to be
opositivo/a HIV positive
vicio, el service charge; service
vicio service
 la habitación room
e lavandería) laundry
if
yes
cómo no! yes, of course!
a, la chair
a de playa, la sun lounger
a de ruedas, la wheelchair
a para niños, la high chair
 without
tomas, los symptoms
ven they serve
o de taxis, el taxi rank
os arqueológicos, los
 rchaeological sites
re, el envelope
retodo, el coat (Arg: for men)
corro! help!
, el sun
o; solamente only
o/a alone; neat
o ocupante single occupancy
cero/a single
nbrilla, la sunshade
nnolencia, la drowsiness
bete, el sorbet
tén, el bra (CAm)
  I am
te, el underground (Arg)
títulos, los subtitles

la de wind-surf, la windsurf board
leta, la tablet
bartería, la handicraft shop (Arg)
a, la size (clothes)
ado/a carved
er, el garage; workshop
naño normal/grande normal/large
ze
nbién also; too
npones, los tampons
ado, el coat (Arg: for women)
adura, la filling (dental) (Mex, Chi)
ete, el rug; carpet
uilla, la ticket office
la x minutos it takes x minutes
e, la afternoon

tarjeta, la card
 postal postcard
 telefónica phone card
tarjeta card
 de crédito/débito credit/debit
 de memoria memory
 de teléfono phone
taxi, el taxi
té de menta, el mint tea (Arg)
teatro, el theatre
tejido/a knitted
telas, las textiles
teléfono, el telephone
televisión, la television
tenemos we've got
tener to have (own)
tengo I've got
tenis, el tennis
termina it finishes
terminal de autobuses, la coach
 station
terminar to finish
término medio medium (steak)
tétano, el tetanus
tianguis, el market (Mex)
tiempo, el time
tienda, la shop; tent
tienda de artesanías, la handicraft
 shop
¿tiene . . . ? do you have . . . ?
tifoidea, la typhoid
timón, el steering wheel
tinto, el black coffee (Col)
típico/a traditional
tipo, el type
toalla, la towel
toallas higiénicas/sanitarias, las
 sanitary towels
todo everything
todo/a(s) all
todos los días every day
tomar to have (food); to take (grab)
topes, los speed bumps
toros, los bullfighting
torre, la tower
tos, la cough
tour, el tour
trabajo, el work; job
tragar to swallow
tráiler, el caravan
tren, el train
trigo, el wheat
trusa, la swimming costume (Cub)
turquesa, la turquoise

U
último/a last

V

va it goes
vacío/a empty
vacunado/a contra vaccinated against
vainilla, la vanilla
valija, la suitcase (Arg)
valor, el value
vararse to break down (Col)
veces, las (tres veces) times (three
  times)
végano/a vegan
vegetariano/a vegetarian
velero, el sailing boat
velocidad, la speed
vender to sell
ventana, la window
ventanilla, la ticket office (Arg)
ventilador, el fan
ver to see
verano, el summer
verdad, la truth
verde green
vestido de baño, el swimming costume
  (Col)
vestidores, los changing rooms
vía cerrada no entry
viajar to travel
viaje, el journey; trip
videojuego portátil, el portable video
  game
vidrio, el glass
viejo/a old
villa (juvenil), la youth hostel
vino, el wine
violar to rape
visita, la visit
visitante, el/la visitor
visor, el diving mask
vista al mar, la sea view
vivir to live
volante, el steering wheel (Mex, SCon)
volar en paracaídas to parasail
volver to return
vomitar to be sick
¡vuelva! come back!

W

whisky (en las rocas), el whisky (on the
  rocks)

Y

¡ya mismo! straight away!

Z

zócalo, el main square (Mex)
zona, la area